An Unhurried View

of COPYRIGHT

BENJAMIN KAPLAN

THE LAWBOOK EXCHANGE, LTD.
Clark, New Jersey
2008

ISBN-13: 978-1-58477-907-0 (cloth)

ISBN-10: 1-58477-907-1 (cloth)

ISBN-13: 978-1-58477-908-7 (paperback)

ISBN-10: 1-58477-908-X (paperback)

This English-language reprint edition is specially authorized by the original Publisher, Columbia University Press.

The quality of this reprint is equivalent to the quality of the original work.

THE LAWBOOK EXCHANGE, LTD.

33 Terminal Avenue

Clark, New Jersey 07066-1321

Please see our website for a selection of our other publications and fine facsimile reprints of classic works of legal history:

www.lawbookexchange.com

Library of Congress Cataloging-in-Publication Data

Kaplan, Benjamin, 1911-
  An unhurried view of copyright / Benjamin Kaplan.
    p. cm.
  Originally published: New York : Columbia University Press, 1967.
  Includes bibliographical references and index.
  ISBN-13: 978-1-58477-907-0 (cloth : alk. paper)
  ISBN-10: 1-58477-907-1 (cloth : alk. paper)
  ISBN-13: 978-1-58477-908-7 (pbk. : alk. paper)
  ISBN-10: 1-58477-908-X (pbk. : alk. paper)
  1. Copyright--United States. I. Title.
  KF2995.K37 2008
  346.7304'82--dc22   2008014731

Printed in the United States of America on acid-free paper

An Unhurried View

of COPYRIGHT

BENJAMIN KAPLAN

COLUMBIA UNIVERSITY PRESS

NEW YORK AND LONDON

JAMES S. CARPENTIER LECTURES

1904-5   JAMES BRYCE, VISCOUNT BRYCE
Law in Its Relation to History

1907-8   JOHN CHIPMAN GRAY
The Nature and Sources of the Law

1910-11   ARTHUR LIONEL SMITH
English Political Writers of the Seventeenth and
Eighteenth Centuries and the Development of Eng-
lish Political Theory from Hobbes to Burke

DAVID JAYNE HILL
The Problem of World Organization as Affected by
the Nature of the Modern State

1911-12   SIR FREDERICK POLLOCK
The Genius of the Common Law

1913-14   SIR COURTENAY ILBERT
The Mechanics of Law Making

1916-17   HAROLD DEXTER HAZELTINE
English Legal History

1919-20   WILLARD BARBOUR
English History with Special Reference to the Development of Rights through Procedure

1923-24   SIR PAUL VINOGRADOFF
Some Problems of Jurisprudence

1926-27   SIR WILLIAM SEARLE HOLDSWORTH
The Historians of Anglo-American Law

1927-28   BENJAMIN NATHAN CARDOZO
The Paradoxes of Legal Science

1940-41   SIR CECIL THOMAS CARR
Aspects of Administrative Law

1955   EDMUND MORRIS MORGAN
Some Problems of Proof under the Anglo-American
System of Litigation

THOMAS REED POWELL
Vagaries and Varieties in Constitutional Interpre-
tation

1956   GLANVILLE WILLIAMS
The Sanctity of Life and the Criminal Law

1962   EDWIN W. PATTERSON
Law in a Scientific Age

1963   ELLIOTT EVANS CHEATHAM
A Lawyer When Needed

1965   LEON RADZINOWICZ
Ideology and Crime

1966   BENJAMIN KAPLAN
An Unhurried View of Copyright

Foreword

THE PROTECTION of property in the products of the mind has
long presented the challenging problem of balancing several
important and competing social interests. Although the number of writers and inventors among us is small, their contribution to the intellectual and material advancement of society
is unique and indispensable. The importance of that contribution was early recognized in the Constitution, in the grant
of power to Congress "To promote the Progress of Science
and useful Arts, by securing for limited Times to Authors
and Inventors the exclusive Right to their respective Writings
and Discoveries." (U.S. Const. Art. I, Sec. 8.) It is significant,
perhaps, that "Authors and Inventors" are the only callings
thus singled out for such special attention, and it is also significant that the need for balancing the interest of the creator
and the interests of society is emphasized in this constitutional
language, which refers to the creator's "exclusive Right" to
his creation, but recognizes the public interest by restricting
the duration of such rights to "limited Times."

Copyright protection became necessary with the invention
of the printing press and had its early beginnings in the
British censorship laws. The fortunes of the law of copyright
have always been closely connected with freedom of expres-

sion, on the one hand, and with technological improvements
in means of dissemination, on the other. Successive ages have
drawn different balances among the interest of the writer in
the control and exploitation of his intellectual property, the
related interest of the publisher, and the competing interest of
society in the untrammeled dissemination of ideas. It is this
striking of balances in the law of copyright in the past, at
present, and for the future, which constitutes the central
theme of the James S. Carpentier Lectures delivered by
Professor Benjamin Kaplan at the Columbia University
School of Law in March, 1966. His counsel that greater
emphasis should be placed on the public's interest in the free
accessibility of ideas is particularly appropriate in an era when
freedom of expression is frequently under attack and when
the means of dissemination of ideas are increasingly concentrated in fewer hands.

The timeliness of Professor Kaplan's analysis of the law of
copyright in the light of technological and social developments
is underscored by current efforts, begun some ten years ago
by the Register of Copyrights, to accomplish a sweeping
revision of our Copyright Law to take into account developments after 1909, when it was last redrawn. Since then, of
course, the phonograph, motion picture, radio, television,
magnetic tape, and other methods of visual and sound reproduction have provided newer, and for some purposes, better
means of dissemination than the printed page. Even more
recently, new aids to dissemination, including the growth of
computer technology, have magnified the problem of control
in securing "exclusive rights," and increased the numbers of
claimants for protection.

Benjamin Kaplan brings a wealth of experience and learning to the analysis of the complex problems involved in the development of copyright. A frequent contributor to legal journals, he brings to the field of protection of literary property scholarly insights gained from several fields of law. An authority on the subject of civil procedure, he made a major contribution to the revision of the Federal Rules as Reporter to the Advisory Committee on Civil Rules, Judicial Conference of the United States. A teacher in the field of copyright and unfair competition at Harvard Law School for many years, he is the coauthor of a widely used and highly regarded casebook on the subject. His acceptance of the Carpentier lectureship was particularly gratifying for the additional reason that it brought back to Columbia Law School an alumnus of the institution ('33) and a former editor-in-chief of its Law Review.

Professor Kaplan's emphasis on the desirability of greater freedom of dissemination of ideas is especially significant because it is at odds with a strong contemporary trend toward more restrictive and longer protection of the exclusive rights of writers and composers. In addressing himself to the challenging issues involved in the protection of literary property, with clarity, erudition, and wit, he renders a special service by questioning some of the timeworn assumptions in the copyright field.

WILLIAM C. WARREN
Dean of the Faculty of Law

Columbia University
1 September 1966

Acknowledgments

FOR advice and criticism, I owe thanks to Oscar H. Davis, Felicia L. Kaplan, Frank I. Michelman, Arthur R. Miller, and Henry J. Steiner. Of course no one is implicated with me in responsibility for the views here expressed.

David P. Griff of the Harvard Law School class of 1967 worked efficiently in helping to prepare the lectures for publication, and Catherine W. Monteiro cheerfully assumed the burden of managing the typescripts.

Lecture III, in somewhat less complete form, was first published in the May 1966 issue of the *Columbia Law Review* (66:831).

B. K.

Chilmark, Mass.
1 September 1966

Contents

Foreword, *by William C. Warren*   vii

Acknowledgments   xi

I. The First Three Hundred Fifty Years   1

II. Plagiarism Reexamined   38

III. Proposals and Prospects   79

Table of Cases Cited   129

Index   137

An Unhurried View of COPYRIGHT

I. The First Three Hundred Fifty Years

AS A veteran listener at many lectures by copyright specialists over the past decade, I know it is almost obligatory for a speaker to begin by invoking the "communications revolution" of our time, then to pronounce upon the inadequacies of the present copyright act, and finally to encourage all hands to cooperate in getting a Revision Bill passed. But as I wish not so much to keep the specialists bemused as to introduce the intelligent general lawyer to the law and mystique of copyright, I think I should begin at an earlier point—the Gutenberg revolution, which started it all.

To strike a personal note, I felt the need to learn about the evolution of copyright when I first read the celebrated opinion of Judge Learned Hand in *Sheldon v. Metro-Goldwyn Pictures Corp.* in 1936.[1] Had the company's movie *Letty Lynton* infringed the play *Dishonored Lady* by Sheldon and Barnes? Both the play and the movie took off from the public domain source of the old Scottish murder trial of Madeleine

[1] 81 F.2d 49 (2d Cir.), *cert. denied*, 298 U.S. 669 (1936).

Smith.[2] The movie was also entitled to make use of a novelized version of that story by Mrs. Belloc Lowndes, since she had given license. But it was claimed that the movie had trespassed on some original elements of the play. So Judge Hand held. The elements consisted of various features of the plot of the play, and a few characterizations. The movie had not copied the dialogue of the play; in many other respects including the dénouement it was quite different from the play.

Now I could see why copying a work word-for-word might be a legal wrong; and no doubt one must go further and punish copying with merely colorable variations. That liability should extend to so indefinite a use or appropriation as seemed to me involved in the *Sheldon* case, however, was not at all obvious or self-proving. I reflected that if man has any "natural" rights, not the least must be a right to imitate his fellows, and thus to reap where he has not sown. Education, after all, proceeds from a kind of mimicry, and "progress," if it is not entirely an illusion, depends on generous indulgence of copying. Thus for me it became a matter of some interest to discover how our law attained to such a result as the *Sheldon* decision.

The object of this lecture is modest: I shall retrace my own search and show you how copyright began and how, under impulsion of various forces, including the economic and the literary, copyright protection extended itself to take in more than the simplest cases of copying.

Caxton founded his press in Westminster in 1476, and soon

---

[2]Madeleine Smith has been recently commemorated by C. Day Lewis in the dramatic monologue "Not Proven," published in his collection REQUIEM FOR THE LIVING 9 (1964).

afterward the Crown began to take an acute interest in this dangerous art and to assert prerogative rights regarding it. A Royal Printer appeared in 1485, and from 1518 onward came a stream of royal grants of privileges and patents for the exclusive printing of particular books or books of stated kinds. With the religious and political upheaval of the Act of Supremacy of 1534, the prerogative was employed in a negative way to impose a general censorship through official licensing.[3] But such a system has always been found a slippery and inefficient business. In a later reign it was thought strategic to enlist in aid of the censorship the covetous self-interest of the very printers and booksellers. When Queen Mary chartered the stationers by letters patent of 4 May 1557,[4] the fellowship, in exchange for the large trade advantages they then secured, undertook to become in practical effect sompnours and pursuivants of the royal censorship, to play the part of "literary constables." Printing was confined to members of the Stationers' Company and such others as might be authorized by the Queen; correspondingly the Master and Wardens of the Company were empowered to search out and seize and destroy illicit presses and unlawful books. In Elizabeth's time the partnership of Company and government for maintaining a closed circle of loyal printers, and for licensing books and otherwise regulating the trade, was articulated in a comprehensive Star Chamber decree of 23 June 1586,[5] said to be the work of Archbishop Whitgift (an unpleasant man). This scheme of the Tudor monarchs—comprising grants of

---

[3]Proclamation of 16 November 1538, reprinted in 1 TUDOR ROYAL PROCLAMATIONS 270 (Hughes & Larkin eds. 1964); see also Proclamation of 8 July 1546, *id.* at 373.

[4]1 ARBER, A TRANSCRIPT OF THE REGISTERS OF THE COMPANY OF STATIONERS OF LONDON xxviii (1875).

[5]2 ARBER, *id.* at 807.

patents for specified works, confinement of printing to authorized presses, licensing of books before publication, use of the
trade organization and special governmental agencies for
enforcement—formed the pattern for subsequent regulatory
efforts right down to the emancipation of the English press
in 1695.[6]

How does all this relate to copyright? To mangle Sir Henry
Maine's aphorism, copyright has the look of being gradually
secreted in the interstices of the censorship. The patents for
books, in that they conferred exclusive rights, bear some
family resemblances to the later legal institution of copyright.
They did not, however, stand on any notion of original composition, for they might be granted for ancient as well as new
works. In the end a large number of patents came into the
hands of the major stationers. Besides the patented books,
books could be published if they were licensed by the official
licensers and printed by an authorized press. A stationer before
proceeding to print must in the usual course of Company
practice obtain allowance from officers of the Company, and
note of the allowance—called entry—was to be made on the
Company's Register. At least among members of the Company
the entry came to betoken ownership of the "copy" of the
book, the exclusive right to print and publish it; in general,
priority of entry spelled priority of right. Some such scheme of
allocation to members was needed for the practical distribution, so to speak, of the authority to print vested in the Company as a community. Again, as between this right of copy by
means of entry and a modern copyright the resemblances are
merely familial: entries were made not only of new but of old

---

[6]The story is summarized in SIEBERT, FREEDOM OF THE PRESS IN ENG-
LAND 1476-1776 (1952).

books. How far a search of the Register was initially made to see whether a proposed entry would infringe on one previously made, we do not know. Various claims of infringement were heard by the Court of Assistants of the Company, and scattered accounts appear in the incomplete records of that court,[7] but the tendency to compromise was so strong that we get little impression of any prevailing notions of piracy or plagiarism. We can, however, surmise that the question would have been viewed with printer's or publisher's not author's eyes. And while there was an idea of piracy of content which might reach beyond verbatim copying,[8] we should not suppose that any abstruse or refined ideas of literary theft could have been entertained.

Right of copy was the stationer's not the author's. Living authors furnished some of the material for the printing mills, and increasingly these manuscripts had to be purchased in a business way (usually payment was made in a lump sum); but upon entry the author dropped away and it was the stationer who had the right of multiplication of copies against others of the Company, which is to say, speaking imprecisely, against all those eligible to print. Augustine Birrell is right to suggest that John Milton was making no declaration for authors' rights when he exclaimed in *Areopagitica* about "the just retaining of each man his several copy, which God forbid should be gainsaid."[9]

The Stationers' Company did by no means go along all

---

[7]RECORDS OF THE COURT OF THE STATIONERS' COMPANY 1576-1602 (Greg & Boswell eds. 1930); *id.* 1602-1640 (Jackson ed. 1957).

[8]See the case of Adams, in Jackson, *supra* at 51, 83, 350, 351; the case of Jaggard, *id.* at 178, *cf.* 204, 326, 327, 328, 334, 335.

[9]MILTON, AREOPAGITICA 50 (Cotterill ed. 1961); BIRRELL, SEVEN LECTURES ON THE LAW AND HISTORY OF COPYRIGHT IN BOOKS 77 (1899).

serene in the retaining of each man his several copy. I shall
forbear an account of the gradual decay of the Company,[10]
and merely make the point that the Company's strength was
dependent in large part upon its alliance with the official
censorship. When, after the Restoration, Parliament in 1662
passed a Printing Act duly restricting printing and reinstalling
licensing,[11] the stationers must dearly have hoped that the
system would stick. It did not. It wobbled and expired
through nonrenewal in 1695. Macaulay, writing deliciously
of the demise of the censorship, shows that it was due to
general disgust at the variable stupidity of the censors.[12]

Three cheers for freedom of the press; but what, now, was
to become of the stationers? Anarchical publication lay ahead
which the stationers, habituated to protection, were not
equipped to meet. So, as Lord Camden later said, "They"—the
stationers, whose property by that time "consisted of all the
literature of the Kingdom; for they had contrived to get all
the copies into their own hands"—"came up to Parliament in
the form of petitioners, with tears in their eyes, hopeless and
forlorn; they brought with them their wives and children to
excite compassion, and induce Parliament to grant them a

[10]See Blagden, The Stationers' Company: A History 1403-1959
(1960).
[11]13 & 14 Car. 2, c. 33.
[12]4 History of England 348-62 (1855). Copyright lawyers may take
wry amusement from the fact that Charles Blount, who by a ruse hoisted
the last official censor, and thus has some claim to be called the liberator of
the English press, was, according to Macaulay, "one of the most unscrupu-
lous plagiaries that ever lived. . . . The literary workmanship of Blount
resembled the architectural workmanship of those barbarians who used the
Coliseum and the Theatre of Pompey as quarries, who built hovels out of
Ionian friezes and propped cowhouses on pillars of lazulite." *Id.* at 354.

statutory security."[13] Whence came the Statute of Anne.[14]

The act secured the existing copy of books already printed for a term of twenty-one years from 10 April 1710. With respect to new books, it vested the copy in the authors or their assigns for a period of fourteen years from the date of publication, with provision for returning the copy to the authors for another term of fourteen years if they should be living when the initial term expired. The copy, according to the statute, was "the sole liberty of printing and reprinting" a book, and this liberty could be infringed by another who should "print, reprint, or import" the book without consent. Offenders were to forfeit their books to the owners of the copy who were forthwith to "damask and make waste paper of them"; and offenders were to forfeit also a penny a sheet, one moiety to the Queen and the other to the person suing for the same. And to prevent infringement through innocent mistake, it was provided that the forfeiture and penalty could not be exacted with respect to new books unless the title to the copy was entered, before publication, in the register book at the Hall of the Stationers' Company. (So passed the ancient glory of the worshipful Company. Only in this ministerial clause, and the further one requiring deposit of specimen books for transmission to the great libraries, was the Company mentioned.)

I doubt that the statute was any more grounded on a thoughtful review of policy than the defeat of official licensing had been. The stationers made the case that they could not produce the fragile commodities called books, and thus en-

[13]Donaldson v. Becket (H.L. 1774), as reported in 17 HANSARD, PARLIA-MENTARY HISTORY OF ENGLAND 953, 995 (1813).
[14]8 Anne, c. 19 (1710).

courage learned men to write them, without protection against
piracy; but no one, we can be sure, deliberated what strange
results might follow if the same logic were applied to other
fragile ventures outside the book field. It is hard to know how
far the interests of authors were considered in distinction from
those of publishers. There is an apparent tracing of rights to
an ultimate source in the fact of authorship, but before
attaching large importance to this we have to note that if
printing as a trade was not to be put back into the hands of a
few as a subject of monopoly—if the statute was indeed to be
a kind of "universal patent"—a draftsman would naturally be
led to express himself in terms of rights in books and hence
of initial rights in authors. A draftsman would anyway be
aware that rights would usually pass immediately to publishers
by assignment, that is, by purchase of the manuscripts as in
the past. (It was held, incidentally, that the possibility of
reversion after the fourteen years could also be assigned.)[15]
Although references in the text of the statute to authors,
together with dubious intimations in later cases that Swift,
Addison, and Steele took some significant part in the drafting,[16]
have lent color to the notion that authors were themselves
intended beneficiaries of the parliamentary grace, I think it
nearer the truth to say that publishers saw the tactical advantage of putting forward authors' interests together with their
own, and this tactic produced some effect on the tone of the

[15]See Fred Fisher Music Co. v. M. Witmark & Sons, 318 U.S. 643, 648
(1943).
[16]See the remarks of counsel for the appellants in Donaldson v. Becket,
2 Bro. P.C. 129, 139, 140, 1 Eng. Rep. 837, 843; and of Lord Chancellor
Apsley in the same case, as reported in 17 HANSARD, *supra* note 13, at 1002.
See also Lord Chief Baron Abinger in D'Almaine v. Boosey, 1 Y. & C. Ex.
288, 299, 160 Eng. Rep. 117, 122 (Ex. 1835).

statute. Next, considering what was thought protectible under the statute and how it was to be protected, I venture to say, first, that the distinction between old and new books was intended or could be easily taken to mean that to qualify for protection as a new book a work must have some ingredient of fresh authorship and be not merely a reissue or, perhaps, not an existing work merely réchauffé—rewarmed. Second, the draftsman was thinking as a printer would—of a book as a physical entity; of rights in it and offenses against it as related to "printing and reprinting" the thing itself; of punishment for illicit reprinting as involving in the first instance destruction of the very duplicating book. But conjectures about what the draftsman may have thought are vain: copyright was now going to be submitted to rationalization by the judges.

The meaning of a statute is apt to be first tested in strange cases on the periphery of the enactment rather than in its heartland. So the first substantial question to arise under the Statute of Anne was that of alleged infringement by translation. Dr. Thomas Burnet's Latin work *Archaeologiae Philosophicae* had been published in 1692 and could presumably claim protection under the statute until 1731. In 1720 the defendants threatened an English translation and when sued in Chancery they justified on the expected ground. The statute, they said, "could be intended only to restrain the mechanical art of printing," but a translation "in some respects may be called a different book, and the translator may be said to be the author, in as much as some skill in language is requisite thereto, and not barely a mechanic art, as in the case of reprinting in the same language." Again, the translator put the book into a different form, and *"forma dat esse rei."*

Finally, a translation was rather within the statute's encouragement of learning than within its prohibition of reprinting.
Lord Chancellor Macclesfield said, "a translation might not
be the same with the reprinting the original, on account that
the translator has bestowed his care and pains upon it"—which
suggested that if the accused book was a work of authorship,
it could not at the same time infringe.[17] The case, however,
went off on an erratic ground.[18]

Twenty years later we have an opinion on the trying question of abridgment, of which the core meaning is (to use an
O.E.D. definition) "a compendium of a larger work, with the
details abridged, and less important things omitted, but retaining the sense and substance." Gyles, a bookseller, claiming
copyright in an edition of Sir Matthew Hale's *Pleas of the
Crown*, sought relief against the book *Modern Crown Law*
alleged to be "colourable only . . . borrowed vertatim . . .
only some old statutes . . . left out which are now repealed;
and . . . all the Latin and French quotations . . . translated
into English." Lord Chancellor Hardwicke framed the question as being whether the defendant's book was "the same
with" the Hale edition. Books only "colourably shortened"
were piracies, according to the Chancellor; "but," said he,
"this must not be carried so far as to restrain persons from
making a real and fair abridgment, for abridgments may with
great propriety be called a new book, because not only the
paper and print, but the invention, learning, and judgment of

    [17]Burnett v. Chetwood, 2 Mer. 441, 35 Eng. Rep. 1008-09 (Ch. 1720).
    [18]The Lord Chancellor thought the book "contained strange notions, in-
tended by the author to be concealed from the vulgar in the Latin language."
In its "superintendency over all books," the court would "restrain the printing or publishing any that contained reflections on religion or morality"—at
least reflections in English! *Ibid.*

the author is shown in them, and in many cases are extremely useful, though in some cases prejudicial, by mistaking and curtailing the sense of an author."[19] So, apparently, we have to look to the nature and extent of the defendant's contribution and, perhaps, also to the question of form. On Lord Hardwicke's suggestion the issue of fair abridgment was referred to arbitration, in which, evidently, the plaintiff failed.[20]

Two more cases on abridgment deserve mention here. Samuel Johnson's *Rasselas* came before the Master of the Rolls, Sir Thomas Clarke, in 1761 on a claim that the defendants had infringed by printing in their *Grand Magazine of Magazines* a part of the narrative, leaving out "all the reflections." Sir Thomas said that on the question of fair abridgment each case must depend on its own circumstances. He then observed that magazines customarily printed abstracts of authors; indeed the plaintiffs had themselves printed an abstract of *Rasselas* in the *London Chronicle*. So business reasoning entered into the dismissal of the bill: the defendants had not interfered unduly with the sale of the book.[21] The second case, evidently to be dated in 1773, is notable for the fact that Lord Chancellor Apsley consulted Justice Blackstone. The defendant Newbery had condensed or abstracted Hawkesworth's *Voyages*—Hawkesworth's authorized reconstruction from original journals of a number of marine exploits including Cook's first circumnavigation of the globe. The Lord Chancellor spoke of change of form, the defendant's

[19]Gyles v. Wilcox, 2 Atk. 141, 3 Atk. 269, 26 Eng. Rep. 489, 957; Barn. Ch. 368, 27 Eng. Rep. 682 (Ch. 1740).
[20]See Tonson v. Walker, 3 Swans. 672, 679, 36 Eng. Rep. 1017, 1020 (Ch. 1752), stating the result of the arbitration.
[21]Dodsley v. Kinnersley, Amb. 403, 27 Eng. Rep. 270 (Ch. 1761).

labor, and advantage to readers. An abridgment preserving "the whole" of a work "in its sense" is "an act of understanding," "in the nature of a new and meritorious work." Newbery was not only exculpated but congratulated for reducing Hawkesworth and preserving the substance in different language perhaps better than the original.[22]

We have now reached the time of the climax of the debate over the greatest of all copyright questions, known as *The* Question of Literary Property, a question which had been stirring since 1731. Private rights could subsist in a work for an indefinite period so long as it remained unpublished and thus outside the range of the Statute of Anne. The question related rather to published works. Did the copyright in published works cease at the expiration of the limited periods specified in the statute, or was there a nonstatutory, common-law copyright of perpetual duration, with the statute merely furnishing accumulative special remedies during the limited periods? In strictness, the embarrassing issue, "wherein consists the identity of a book,"[23] need not have been faced in any of the relevant litigations, for the accused works were word-for-word copies and thus clear piracies if copyright on any terms survived the statutory periods. But practically the issue could not be avoided: a right without limit of time was being claimed, and its horizontal dimension, so to speak, was plainly important. Proponents would be intent to show that

[22]Newbery's Case, Lofft 775, 98 Eng. Rep. 913 (Ch. 1773). For a recent low estimate of the quality of Hawkesworth's writing, see BYRON'S JOURNAL OF HIS CIRCUMNAVIGATION 1764-1766 (Gallagher ed. 1964), intro. at lxxvi-lxxxii.

[23]See Willes, J., in Millar v. Taylor, 4 Burr. 2303, 2310, 98 Eng. Rep. 201, 205 (K.B. 1769).

the perpetual right was narrow enough to be tolerable, while opponents would try to show its inordinate potential breadth as a reason for denying its existence in the first place. So argument proceeded on the shape of copyright considered as property rather than as a mere statutory construct—*propriété* rather than *privilège*, as the French would say.

Lord Mansfield was the brightest intelligence on the side of the respectable stationers. He had appeared as their counsel in the inconclusive first two *Tonson* cases involving works of John Milton, "old books" whose copyright had expired under the statute in 1731.[24] Becoming Chief Justice of King's Bench, Mansfield presided in the aborted third *Tonson* case involving *Spectators* originally published in 1711—"new books."[25] Then came the litigation over James Thomson's *The Seasons,* also a "new book," first published in 1727–30. Under the title *Millar v. Taylor,* King's Bench in 1769 held for the perpetual right.[26] Mansfield spoke himself in judgment, and his voice can also be heard in the remarks of the side Justices Willes and Aston. Mansfield stressed the essential "decency" of securing for the author the opportunity to recover his expenses and earn a profit, the right to decide how his name and work should be presented to the public. (The fact that publishers, not authors, were at bar, was passed over in silence, as usual.) On the dimension of the perpetual right, Mansfield seemed to revert

[24]Tonson v. Walker (Ch. 1739), referred to at 4 Burr. 2325, 98 Eng. Rep. 213; Tonson v. Walker, 3 Swans. 672, 36 Eng. Rep. 1017 (Ch. 1752).
[25]Tonson v. Collins, 1 Black. W. 301, 96 Eng. Rep. 169 (K.B. 1761).
[26]4 Burr. 2303, 98 Eng. Rep. 201 (K.B. 1769). *The Seasons* of course has figured heavily not only in legal but in literary history. See the analysis of the critical appreciation of the poem over the past two centuries in Professor Ralph Cohen's book THE ART OF DISCRIMINATION: THOMSON'S THE SEASONS AND THE LANGUAGE OF CRITICISM (1964).

to the printer's old right of copy, "an incorporeal right to
the sole printing and publishing of somewhat intellectual,
communicated by letters." Copyright of a work did not bar
others from using it, still less from dealing with the same
subject matter; rather it barred them from reproducing a
similar text. Justice Willes accepted that copyright did not
prevent "bona fide imitations, translations, and abridgments";
a book "conveys knowledge, instruction, or entertainment;
but multiplying copies in print is quite a distinct thing from
all the book communicates. And there is no incongruity, to
reserve that right; and yet convey the free use of all the book
teaches." Justice Aston said that a man who bought a published work "may improve upon it, imitate it, translate it;
oppose its sentiments: but he buys no right to publish the
identical work."

Lord Mansfield did not produce his usual mesmeric effect
on the other associate Justice, Yates,[27] who, dissenting in the
Millar case, argued that if a copyright could exist at common
law it must go the length of protecting the ideas of the work;
but these were "quite wild," incapable of *indicia certa*. The
theme was taken up and embroidered in *Donaldson v.
Becket*,[28] an appeal to the House of Lords from an injunction
which had been granted by Chancery, on the strength of the
law judgment in the *Millar* case, against the unlicensed
reprinting and sale of *The Seasons* by the daring Scottish
bookseller Donaldson. Submitting his opinion to the Lords,

[27]Yates had been of counsel for the defendant in the third Tonson case,
supra note 25. For his feelings toward Mansfield when they both sat in
King's Bench, see FIFOOT, LORD MANSFIELD 47 (1936).
    [28]2 Bro. P.C. 129, 1 Eng. Rep. 837, 4 Burr. 2408, 98 Eng. Rep. 257
(H.L. 1774), 17 HANSARD, PARLIAMENTARY HISTORY OF ENGLAND 953-
1003 (1813).

Chief Justice DeGrey of Common Pleas suggested that the Mansfield position was self-contradictory, for if a common-law perpetuity could indeed be raised upon "an equitable and moral right," "abridgments of books, translations, notes" must figure as infringements, for these "as effectually deprive the original author of the fruit of his labours, as direct particular copies. . . ."[29] And what of mechanical inventions generally, as to which, it was pretty well conceded by the Mansfield school, no tenable argument of common-law perpetuity could be made?[30] Similarly Lord Camden questioned what would be exempt from the "desultory claim"[31] which must underlie the injunction appealed from. Would it not, horrible thought, take in, as infringements, translations and abridgments as well as lending out of books or transcribing them even for charity?

The *Donaldson* appeal succeeded in 1774 and the common-law perpetuity was repelled and denied.[32] Conceivably judges

---

[29] 17 HANSARD, *supra* note 28, at 990.

[30] Fending off the analogy to mechanical invention, Justice Aston had said in the Millar case—rather lamely, it must be owned—that a machine made in imitation of another was necessarily different in "substance, materials, labour and expence," while a "reprinted book is the very same substance," the printing being "the method only of publishing and promulgating the contents of the book." 4 Burr. at 2348, 98 Eng. Rep. at 226. This distinction was early suggested by Bishop Warburton and recurs in the debates on the question of the perpetual right. See Blackstone's argument as counsel for the plaintiff in Tonson v. Collins, 1 Black. W. 301, 343, 96 Eng. Rep. 169, 189 (K.B. 1761).

[31] 17 HANSARD, supra note 28, at 998.

[32] The wiser heads acquiesced in the denial of the perpetuity, although some thought the term of the Statute of Anne was too short. See Samuel Johnson to the publisher William Strahan, 7 March 1774, in 1 CHAPMAN, THE LETTERS OF SAMUEL JOHNSON 398 (1952); David Hume to Strahan, ascribed to Spring 1774, in HILL, LETTERS OF DAVID HUME TO WILLIAM STRAHAN 274 (1888); see also Hume to Strahan, 2 April 1774, *id.* at 280.

might be led to give generous horizontal scope to a copyright which was now definitely short-lived. On the other hand, the *Donaldson* decision centered attention on the text of the Statute of Anne as being the source of rights in published works, and that seemed to provide merely a counterpart to the old right of copy.

We hear finally from Lord Mansfield in *Sayre v. Moore*.[33] Sitting at Guildhall in 1785, he tried this action under a statute covering maps and charts as copyrightable subject matter.[34] The plaintiff, "laying down" from extant charts and resorting to printed and manuscript accounts of travelers, had prepared and published at considerable expense four sea charts. The defendant had combined the four charts into one, on which he corrected some soundings and, evidently applying the Mercator principle, corrected latitudes and longitudes, thus rendering the whole more useful to navigation. Here was a difficult problem for which the earlier debates, which had chiefly in mind literary works of imagination, had made no room. Maps necessarily resemble one another in form, the more so as they accurately picture the reality. So form could not be the key to copyrightability or infringement. To require a map maker in 1785 to forbear the sedulous use of the earlier art might be not only impractical but dangerous. In the translation and abridgment cases the defendants had escaped infringement by contributing "somewhat intellectual" notwithstanding they had used the plaintiffs' works pervasive-

---

[33]1 East 361 n., 102 Eng. Rep. 139 n. (K.B. 1785). The judgment by Mansfield in Bach v. Longman, 2 Cowp. 623, 98 Eng. Rep. 1274 (K.B. 1777), holding a musical composition to be a writing within the Statute of Anne, is also of some interest.

[34]See 7 Geo. 3, c. 38 (1766); 17 Geo. 3, c. 57 (1777).

ly. Lord Mansfield said: "whoever has it in his intention to publish a chart may take advantage of all prior publications." Was the accused map a "servile imitation" or something more? Here it embodied alterations and corrected errors. "If an erroneous chart be made, God forbid it should not be corrected even in a small degree." On such a charge, the jury was for the defendant.

Lord Mansfield had begun in the *Sayre* case with the famous passage: "we must take care to guard against two extremes equally prejudicial; the one, that men of ability, who have employed their time for the service of the community, may not be deprived of their just merits, and the reward of their ingenuity and labour; the other, that the world may not be deprived of improvements, nor the progress of the arts be retarded." Recalling the decisions so far, we can say that the infringement problem was being answered, seventy-five years after the basic statute, by looking not so much to what the defendant had taken as to what he had added or contributed. And the treatment of the abstract of *Rasselas* suggested that even a bodily taking without addition or improvement could be defended if it was conceived not to interfere unduly with the normal economic exploitation of the copyright.

In the *Sayre* opinion, histories and dictionaries were mentioned as being analogous to maps. Distinctions, however, might be taken. Change of form might be required as a condition of lifting from histories and even from dictionaries, but could not be feasibly demanded in the case of maps. And though amplified or corrected maps must usually be published entire, one might be able to insist, as to informational works

in literary form, that the later author publish only his additions or changes and steer clear of duplicating the original.
Yet if the logic of the *Sayre* case was accepted, it would seem
pointless or stultifying to require either device as a means
of avoiding infringement, and the *Sayre* case therefore did
seem to look to easy appropriation from any informational work
if the later author added some significant elements of information.

Now in the period between the *Sayre* decision and the
recodification of copyright law by the first Victorian statute of
1842, the English courts dealt repeatedly with informational
works ranging from roadbooks and directories to commonplace
histories and treatises. And Lord Mansfield's opinion was soon
brought into question.

A bare four years after the *Sayre* case, Lord Kenyon tried
Trusler v. Murray,[35] an action for pirating a book of chronology. We are told that "though some parts of the defendant's
work were different, yet in general it was the same, and particularly from page 20 to 34 it was a literal copy." Lord Kenyon
said, "if such were the fact"—presumably referring to the
fourteen pages—the defendant was liable "though other parts
of the [defendant's] work were original."[36] Possible conflict
with the *Sayre* case arose if the chronology was thought of as
a compilation of facts on which the defendant had engrafted
factual changes or additions of consequence. The issue between Kenyon and Mansfield was put thus in the argument

[35]1 East 362 n., 102 Eng. Rep. 140 n. (K.B. 1789). Lord Kenyon seems
to misconceive the result in Newbery's Case, *supra* note 22, regarding the
abridgment of Hawkesworth's *Voyages*.

[36]By agreement, the matter was submitted to arbitration. It is reported in
Matthewson v. Stockdale, 12 Ves. Jun. 270, 273, 33 Eng. Rep. 103, 104
(Ch. 1806), that the plaintiff prevailed.

of counsel for defendant in a later case involving an East India calendar: "either the public cannot have the corrections; or the author of them must include the original work in his."[37]

The question, however, was not squarely faced; the course of decision was ambiguous and halting.[38] Lord Chancellor Erskine showed a certain sensitivity to the point.[39] Finally Lord Chancellor Eldon, a great vacillator, did move, if I read him aright, to a formulation distinct from Mansfield's. The break perhaps comes in *Longman v. Winchester* in 1809.[40] The defendant's "Imperial Calendar" absorbed much of the information in the plaintiff's elaborate calendar or directory, but it evidently made additions and corrections. Lord Eldon bore down on the fact that the defendant had availed himself of the plaintiff's labor; he had not replowed the field. The plaintiff to the extent of his independent labor could hold a copyright, and the defendant in the degree that he leaned on the plaintiff's labor was an infringer. Lord Eldon did not say whether the defendant had altered the form of presentation, nor did he comment on the significance of form.

The trend away from the position I have ascribed to Mansfield continued, although with lapses, in the decisions of the

[37]Matthewson v. Stockdale, *supra* note 36, 12 Ves. Jun. at 272, 33 Eng. Rep. at 104.

[38]Note the curious perversities of the roadbook cases, Carnan v. Bowles, 2 Bro. C.C. 80, 29 Eng. Rep. 45 (Ch. 1786); Cary v. Faden, 5 Ves. Jun. 24, 31 Eng. Rep. 453 (Ch. 1799); Cary v. Longman, 1 East 358, 102 Eng. Rep. 138 (K.B. 1801); Cary v. Kearsley, 4 Esp. 168, 170 Eng. Rep. 679 (K.B. 1802).

[39]See his judgment in Matthewson v. Stockdale, *supra* note 36, continuing an injunction after an earnest but futile search for additions or improvements.

[40]16 Ves. Jun. 269, 33 Eng. Rep. 987 (Ch. 1809).

next thirty years on informational works.[41] And the notion of prohibited taking became more sophisticated. Lord Chancellor Cottenham developed the thought—which soon influenced Justice Story in a leading American case[42]—that the question of the substantiality of an infringement was not necessarily a quantitative matter but might involve a qualitative judgment as to the importance of the part appropriated.[43] Then we have the expansive notions suggested by legislation adopted to reach works outside the book field. Thus the act on engravings prohibited copying "in whole or in part, by varying, adding to, or diminishing from the main design"[44] (compare this with the simple printing-reprinting formula of the Statute of Anne). We find one court prepared to hold a defendant liable where he had followed the plaintiff's design as a model but changed the embellishments materially;[45] a judge in another case defined "copy" as "that which comes so near to the original as to give every person seeing it *the idea* created by the original."[46] In like spirit was the analysis in *D'Almaine v. Boosey*,

[41] See Mawman v. Tegg, 2 Russ. 385, 38 Eng. Rep. 380 (Ch. 1826); Nichols v. Loder, 2 Coop. T. Cott. 217, 47 Eng. Rep. 1135 (Ch. 1831); Bramwell v. Halcomb, 2 My. & Cr. 737, 40 Eng. Rep. 1110 (Ch. 1836); Lewis v. Fullarton, 2 Beav. 6, 48 Eng. Rep. 1080 (Ch. 1839); Kelly v. Hooper, 1 Y. & C.C.C. 197, 62 Eng. Rep. 852 (1841). Many years later Scrutton could still say: "The English law lays too much stress on new matter added, too little on old matter taken." SCRUTTON, COPYRIGHT 144 (4th ed. 1903).

[42] Gray v. Russell, 10 Fed. Cas. 1035, 1039 (No. 5728) (C.C.D.Mass. 1839).

[43] Bramwell v. Halcomb, 2 My. & Cr. 737, 40 Eng. Rep. 1110 (Ch. 1836).

[44] 8 Geo. 2, c. 13, §1 (1735).

[45] Roworth v. Wilkes, 1 Camp. 94, 170 Eng. Rep. 889 (K.B. 1807). This, however, involved illustrations of standard fencing positions. The defendant had allegedly represented the same figures, "but disguised by a different costume."

[46] West v. Francis, 5 B. & Ald. 737, 743, 106 Eng. Rep. 1361, 1363 (K.B. 1822) (italics in text supplied).

the first important treatment of musical infringement. The defendant had taken certain airs of Auber's opera *Lestocq* and reset or rearranged them for dances as quadrilles and waltzes. Vainly did the defendant argue on analogy to abridgment. "Substantially," said Lord Chief Baron Abinger, "the piracy is where the appropriated music, though adapted to a different purpose from that of the original, may still be recognized by the ear. The adding variations makes no difference in the principle."[47]

If an "improvement" by the defendant could not justify a substantial direct taking, as the *Longman* calendar case taught, what might justify such a taking? Lord Eldon ruminated in *Wilkins v. Aikin*[48] about the hypothetical case of a man writing a history of the mapping of Middlesex who reproduced maps published by another. Eldon suggested that if the taking were for the purpose merely of illustrating the history, it might be permissible; but the decision would be different if under color of a cartographic history the copyist sought to make a profit from republishing the maps themselves. This recalls the dispute over the abstract of *Rasselas* and hints at a modern doctrine sometimes called "fair use." Some other references to appropriations defensible because of the peculiar uses to which they were put appeared in the cases;[49] it was common ground that quotation could be justified when needed for criticism or review.[50]

Despite the reshuffling of doctrine which I have just

[47]1 Y. & C. Ex. 288, 302, 160 Eng. Rep. 117, 123 (Ex. 1835).
[48]17 Ves. Jun. 422, 34 Eng. Rep. 163 (Ch. 1810).
[49]See, *e.g.*, Martin v. Wright, 6 Sim. 297, 58 Eng. Rep. 605 (Ch. 1833); Saunders v. Smith, 3 My. & Cr. 711, 40 Eng. Rep. 1100 (Ch. 1838).
[50]Bell v. Whitehead, 3 Jur. 68 (Ch. 1839).

described, the translation and abridgment rules continued undisturbed. I find no exactly pertinent case on a translation,[51] but cases did continue to arise on abridgments. It should perhaps be noted that the freedom of a magazine to publish an outline of the plot of a current play (the *corpus delicti* was Poole's *Who's Who, or The Double Imposture*) was accepted as a matter of course, evidently as a situation well within the abridgment rule.[52]

The developments after Mansfield looking in the main to enlarged copyright protection were not, I suggest, merely spun out of logical analysis. They reflected great environmental changes—social and economic changes, changes in the literary and artistic outlook.

An indulgent attitude toward using other people's works seemed increasingly out of keeping with the realities of the market. The business of publishing and distributing books had become bigger, more competitive, more impersonal; the stakes were higher, the risks more serious. In this atmosphere there would be ever greater anxiety about marking out metes and bounds of literary ownership, and courts might be expected to respond to arguments about protection of investment.

With the decline of patronage, writers had to stand on their own feet; and as a reading public grew, writers began to feel themselves members of a professional class, and occasionally to speak out with their own demands for recog-

---

[51]It was held that a translation could itself hold a copyright, Wyatt v. Barnard, 3 Ves. & B. 77, 35 Eng. Rep. 408 (Ch. 1814), but that was distinct from the question whether an unlicensed translation of a copyrighted work was an infringement. See also Murray v. Bogue, 1 Drew. 353, 61 Eng. Rep. 487 (Ch. 1852).

[52]Whittingham v. Wooler, 2 Swans. 428, 36 Eng. Rep. 679 (Ch. 1817).

nition and protection.[53] Emergence of the professional man of letters in our modern sense had indeed been delayed not advanced by the Restoration, as the critic Beljame has shown;[54] but if Dryden was not the first such figure, Pope does so qualify.

Literary criticism became less friendly to imitation. The classical or neoclassical attitude was still dominant when Mansfield flourished, but it was being modified gradually by conceptions anticipating the Romantic revival. Edward Young's *Conjectures on Original Composition*, that wondrous effulgence from a dark poet, was written in 1759, and Young's appeal for a new kind of genius seemed to be answered by Shelley and Keats after the turn of the century.

From the classical writers, as expounded by critics of the Italian and French Renaissance, the Elizabethans had received the notion that artistic excellence lay in imitating the best works of the past, not in attempting free invention.[55] All the needed, indeed all the possible, subjects and materials for literary production were already disclosed in existing writings, the *"publica materies"* to which Horace referred.[56] What was required of an author was to give to the old materials an expression compatible with his own time. To be sure, servile imitation was not admired. The author must select and rein-

---

[53]On the changing conditions of publishing and authorship, see MILLER, THE PROFESSIONAL WRITER IN ELIZABETHAN ENGLAND (1959); COLLINS, AUTHORSHIP IN THE DAYS OF JOHNSON (1959); COCHRANE, DR. JOHNSON'S PRINTER: THE LIFE OF WILLIAM STRAHAN (1964); BARNES, FREE TRADE IN BOOKS: A STUDY OF THE LONDON BOOK TRADE SINCE 1800 (1964).

[54]BELJAME, MEN OF LETTERS AND THE ENGLISH PUBLIC IN THE EIGHT-EENTH CENTURY 1660-1744 (Eng. ed. by Dobrée 1948).

[55]See, generally, WHITE, PLAGIARISM AND IMITATION DURING THE ENGLISH RENAISSANCE (1935).

[56]ARS POETICA, l. 131.

terpret; here lay the improvement which was uniquely his, but which could be levied on in a similar way by later authors. The author was not, like a crow, to try to patch up a disguise with peacock's feathers; like a bee he must steal, but then he must transform, the sweetness of the flowers. Still, in the final count, imitation was essential; innovation was dangerous. The classical doctrine of imitation, as well as imitative practice in and out of conformity with the classical ideal, persisted long after Elizabethan times; and it is not hard to find a correspondence between Mansfield's narrow view of plagiarism and the definition that was supplied, although for a different purpose, by the classical teaching.

Now Edward Young and those who followed spoke for original as against imitative genius, for innovation as desirable in itself. The literary hero is one who, having little learning or disdaining whatever learning he has, takes a fresh look at nature and feeds his art direct from that source. The confrontation must be personal, not filtered through past authority. Bacon's formula for scientific invention is to be applied to literary and artistic composition: let the artist strive to know and revere himself, let him have confidence in his own power to create, as some primordial ancestor must have done before there was any authority to go by. In placing a high value on originality, the new literary criticism, I suggest, tended to justify strong protection of intellectual structures in some respect "new," to encourage a more suspicious search for appropriations even of the less obvious types, and to condemn these more roundly when found.[57] It may be objected that Romantic literary ideas have little relevance to the class of pedestrian,

[57] *Cf.* Umbreit, *A Consideration of Copyright,* 87 U. PA. L. REV. 932, 947-48 (1939).

nonimaginative works which was the main subject of copyright litigation. But this category cannot be marked off clearly
from the other; and the courts traditionally have not been careful to distinguish the various classes of works on functional
grounds. It is also possible that the easy business appeal for
liability of cases of pilfering compilations or the like carried
over to works of higher literary quality. In all events we are
dealing with forces that worked themselves out over a long
period of time, and not in an even flow.

The year 1830 or thereabouts is the right time to take leave
of Westminster Hall and visit the United States. Previous
events in this country can be quickly sketched in. By the time
of the Constitutional Convention the original states excepting
Delaware had passed copyright laws.[58] But as Madison later
explained in *Federalist No. 43*, the states could not "separately
make effectual provision" for copyright or patent. Hence article I, section 8, clause 8 of the Constitution. Evidently viewing the copyright-patent incentive or "headstart" as a means of
releasing the energies of creative workers, the clause provides
in a pure attractive style that "The Congress shall have Power
. . . To promote the Progress of Science and useful Arts, by
securing for limited Times to Authors and Inventors the exclusive Right to their respective Writings and Discoveries."
The first national copyright act, resembling the Statute of
Anne except in formal details, was approved by President
Washington on 31 May 1790.[59]

[58]Collected in Copyright Enactments of the United States 1783-
1906 (Copyright Office Bull. No. 3, 1906), pp. 11-31.
[59]Act of 31 May 1790, ch. 15, 1 Stat. 124. The act covered books, maps,
and charts.

History plagiarized itself by bringing to our Supreme Court a dispute on the lines of *Donaldson v. Becket*. This was *Wheaton v. Peters*,[60] a suit upon Wheaton's contributions as reporter to certain volumes of Supreme Court reports bearing his name, infringed, so it was claimed, by Peters's *Condensed Reports*. The bill was framed as well upon the common law as the statute; this caution was used because, of the four formal steps prescribed for going under the statute[61]—recording the title, inscribing the record in the book, advertising the record in newspapers, delivering a copy of the book to the Secretary of State—there was doubt whether the two latter steps had actually been taken with respect to the Wheaton volumes. As the statutory period of protection on those books had not expired, the *Donaldson* question of a right without limit of time could have been avoided by following English authority to the effect that failure to satisfy a formality—registration at Stationers' Hall—merely defeated recovery of the statutory penalties for infringement and left intact claims for general relief.[62] But counsel and the Court went far more broadly; the opinions review The Question of Literary Property; and it was held— out-Englishing the English—that copyright was a statutory construct to the point of demanding exact compliance with the formalities as a condition of any protection for a published

[60]33 U.S. (8 Pet.) 591 (1834). McLean, J., wrote for the Court. Thompson and Baldwin, JJ., dissented. Baldwin's text does not appear in the first or second edition of 8 Peters, but may be found in the third edition by Frederick C. Brightly, New York 1884.

[61]Including an amendatory Act of 29 April 1802, ch. 36, 2 Stat. 171.

[62]See Beckford v. Hood, 7 T.R. 620, 101 Eng. Rep. 1164 (K.B. 1798). The result of this case was apparently confirmed by 41 Geo. 3, c. 107, esp. §§ 1, 4 (1801).

book.[63] American law thus started from the same baseline as the English, but with us there was added an insistence on punctilios which has continued, with occasional displays almost of savagery in forfeiting copyrights, down to recent days. As the formalities had to be carried out around the time of publication, the hazards became aggravated by growing uncertainties about when, in legal contemplation, a work was "published." Indeed the whole concept of publication, fundamental to the operation of the statute, which for the most part treated of published not unpublished works, suffered over the years from a growing assortment of complexities.[64]

Chief American expositor and reinterpreter of English copyright doctrine was Joseph Story. Between 1839 and 1845 he dealt as Circuit Justice with books not quite of the type of roadbooks and directories but still the result more of industrious collection than imagination: one case arose on grammars, another on a biography drawing on an earlier compendium, a third on arithmetics.[65] In these opinions, as well as in his treatise *Equity Jurisprudence*,[66] Story spoke in terms congenial

[63]In yet another sense the Supreme Court went beyond the English. A 7-4 majority of the judges advising the House of Lords on the Donaldson appeal resolved that the author had a post-publication right at common law, but a 6-5 majority resolved that that common-law right was taken away by the Statute of Anne and the statutory right substituted. Professor Nimmer cogently reminds us (NIMMER, COPYRIGHT §47.3 [1963]) that our Supreme Court not only scouted the former resolution but said that, even if correct for England, it did not hold for Pennsylvania, the locus of the Wheaton dispute. See 33 U.S. (8 Pet.) at 658-61.

[64]See *infra*, Lecture III, pp. 83-85.

[65]Gray v. Russell, 10 Fed. Cas. 1035 (No. 5728) (C.C.D.Mass. 1839); Folsom v. Marsh, 9 Fed. Cas. 342 (No. 4901) (C.C.D.Mass. 1841); Emerson v. Davies, 8 Fed. Cas. 615 (No. 4436) (C.C.D.Mass. 1845).

[66]See §§ 930-43 (3d ed. 1843).

to Eldon but carrying his own inflections. Thus he said that an author working with old materials could achieve copyright of his distinctive selection, combination, or arrangement of the components: a later writer infringed if he took this contribution in a substantial degree, though he remained free to rework the old materials in his own way. Such a taking was proscribed even if some fresh improvements were added.[67] Justice Story proceeded to further refinements. He apparently considered that a plan or scheme of presentation or instruction—as found, say, in a school text—having some pretensions to freshness could itself claim protection: to copy the plan might constitute infringement even if the illustrative details had been altered.[68]

But as copyrightability or infringement began to rest on more than the mere matching of word sequences, the abridgment cases looked out-of-line. Story led no assault on the established English doctrine. Rather he seems to have tried to absorb those cases, as reinterpreted, into a general conception of fair use (still unlabeled as such), that is, to read them as a species of the genus of excused appropriation. In *Folsom v. Marsh*, in which he ultimately found infringement in the defendant's biography of Washington culled from Jared Sparks's compendious work *The Writings of George Washington*, Justice Story enumerated factors bearing on privilege or excuse: "the nature and objects of the selections made, the quantity and value of the materials used, and the degree in which the use may prejudice the sale, or diminish the profits, or supersede the objects, of the original work."[69]

[67]Gray v. Russell, 10 Fed. Cas. at 1038.
[68]Emerson v. Davies, 8 Fed. Cas. at 620.
[69]9 Fed. Cas. at 348. See also EQUITY JURISPRUDENCE §§ 939, 940, 942 (3d ed. 1843).

Later judges did not quite understand the point of Story's gingerly handling of abridgments. In 1847, within two years of Story's death, Justice McLean on circuit held an abridgment of Story's own *Equity Jurisprudence* to be in large part fair and noninfringing.[70] McLean's discussion was hardly as delicate as Story's. He yielded to what he took to be settled English law, but he said he disbelieved the cheerful assertions that abridgments did not really interfere with sales of the originals. He went so far as to suggest that, on analogy to patent doctrine, any book using the "principle" of a prior copyrighted work should be held an infringement.[71]

As to translations—on which Justice Story had said very little[72]—there is a flat decision by Justice Grier in 1853 holding that a rendering in German of the full text of *Uncle Tom's Cabin* did not infringe the copyright.[73] Despite developments since the turn of the century, the Justice clung to the notion of copyright as protecting only the very book, the precise concrete expression. Mansfield, Willes, and Aston were duly cited. Like an abridgment, a translation was a "new" book. The fact that a translation of a work out of copyright was sufficiently new to claim copyright—as had been earlier decided[74]—was offered by the defendant's counsel as proof that a translation could not infringe a copyrighted original, and Justice Grier apparently followed his notion that there could be "no hybrid between a thief and a thinker."[75] Justice Grier said that to

[70]Story's Executors v. Holcomb, 23 Fed. Cas. 171 (No. 13497) (C.C.D. Ohio 1847).
[71]23 Fed. Cas. at 172-73.
[72]There is a bland passage in Emerson v. Davies, 8 Fed. Cas. at 619.
[73]Stowe v. Thomas, 23 Fed. Cas. 201 (No. 13514) (C.C.E.D.Pa. 1853).
[74]See *supra* note 51.
[75]23 Fed. Cas. at 205-06.

hold a translation infringing would be wrong on just the ground that it would make a copyright as broad as a patent.

The contretemps about patent was illustrative of the sporadic confusing injection into copyright analysis of oddments reminiscent of patent law: for example, the idea that an author could infringe by devising material which was in fact anticipated in another work though the author did not know of it;[76] or the idea that to attain copyright an author must necessarily exhibit more than the ability of a mere mechanic of the art, as an inventor must show more than ordinary workman's skill.[77] Some basic distinctions were not firmly taken until after the codification of 1909.

Justice Grier's opinion in the case of *Uncle Tom's Cabin* ended with the sweeping statement that by publication of the book all of Mrs. Stowe's "conceptions and inventions" not excepting her characters were made free to the world and could be "used and abused" by playwrights among others.[78] That proposition might be congenial to Mansfield; but was it any longer correct? Was it any longer clear that the story-line of a novel or the plot of a play apart from the specific envelope of narration or dialogue was incapable of protection? An argument the other way, besides drawing on the cases on informational works, could now build on a few decisions about music and graphic art, could appeal to patent doctrine, could

[76]See Hein v. Harris, 183 Fed. 107, 108-09 (2d Cir. 1910), where this proposition was related to the statutory language vesting in the copyright proprietor the "sole liberty" of printing and reprinting the work. See *infra*, Lecture II, pp. 41-43.

[77]See Jollie v. Jaques, 13 Fed. Cas. 910, 913 (No. 7437) (C.C.S.D.N.Y. 1850); *but cf.* Henderson v. Tompkins, 60 Fed. 758, 764 (C.C.D.Mass. 1894).

[78]23 Fed. Cas. at 208.

urge an analogy to Story's recognition of distinctive selection, arrangement, combination, and plan as copyrightable elements. The claim for plot could perhaps be made most effectively with regard to live drama. Shortly after Mrs. Stowe's disappointment, the act of 1856 added an exclusive public performance right as an incident of the copyright of a published dramatic composition,[79] and here a test arose. The case was *Daly v. Palmer*.[80]

The railroad episode at the end of the third scene of the fourth act of *Under the Gaslight*, by Augustin Daly, was popular with audiences, and the defendant sought to use a variant of it in the play *After Dark*, by Dion Boucicault, which was otherwise a quite different work. Both scenes hung on how, or whether, a character tied to the track was to escape an onrushing train; but the precise incidents diverged, as did the speeches. Much of the interest must have derived from the mechanical stage effects, in which copyright was evidently not claimed; for the rest, one would have thought the plaintiff would be hard put to show distinctiveness in the elements of the episode or their combination, and Boucicault had, after all, made changes. The defendant's attempt to show anticipation in prior works—again the hint of patent—was, however, rather feeble, and the court said the "originality and novelty"[81] of plaintiff's scene had not been disproved. Relying on the music case of *D'Almaine v. Boosey*[82] and recalling Story's discussion in the case of arithmetics, the court

[79] Act of 18 August 1856, ch. 169, 11 Stat. 138.

[80] 6 Fed. Cas. 1132 (No. 3552) (C.C.S.D.N.Y. 1868). See also Daly v. Webster, 56 Fed. 483 (2d Cir. 1892); Brady v. Daly, 175 U.S. 148 (1899).

[81] 6 Fed. Cas. at 1138.

[82] See *supra* note 47 and accompanying text.

enjoined the defendant. We shall never know how far the court was yielding to the presumably irrelevant but poignant fact that the defendant was trying to work the lode of spectacular rescue that the plaintiff had proved to be rich in audience appeal, and was planning to open his show in direct competition with the plaintiff's in New York. Writing in the *American Law Review*, defendant's counsel Mr. T. W. Clarke lamented that this "is the first decision which has established a property in incident."[83] He said also that the decision "may be said to advance in literary law the doctrine of romantic[84] equivalents, analogous to the doctrine of mechanical equivalents of the patent or mechanical law." Here, I take it, Mr. Clarke was complaining that mere similarity of impression or effect was being accepted as sufficient to make out infringement.

In 1870 the statute was amended to allow authors to reserve the right not only to translate their works (*pace* Justice Grier) but also to dramatize them.[85] The latter enlargement of the monopoly to cover the conversion of a work from one to another artistic medium, taken together with the *Daly* decision, put the question whether any line could really be held, even as to imaginative works, between "idea," long supposed to be outside copyright protection, and "form," assumed to be the only thing within it. Was a copyrighted work now to be protected according to its "principle," as McLean thought it should be? The question will recur.

At this point I have to mention a kind of counter theme

---

[83]3 Am. L. Rev. 453 (1869). A handwritten annotation by J. C. Gray in his copy of the Review (now in the Harvard Law Library) attributes the comment to Clarke.

[84]The word appears with a lower-case *r*.

[85]Act of 8 July 1870, ch. 230, § 86, 16 Stat. 198.

sounded by the famous case of *Baker v. Selden*.[86] One Selden, in a number of copyrighted books, had described a peculiar system of bookkeeping and had set out blanks and forms intrinsic to it. He had in effect licensed others to use his forms and thus his system; whereupon the defendant Baker began to sell similar forms, working the same system, to bookkeepers and auditors. You will have guessed that Selden failed in the lawsuit; but then the thought will occur to you that the plan of presentation of a grammar or arithmetic, the plot of a play, is a kind of system; and, beyond that, what of the forms themselves as combinations of words and signs? Justice Bradley for the Supreme Court distinguished between Selden's books and the system which they described. Another book about bookkeeping tracking Selden's books would infringe them; but anyone was free to use the system disclosed, in the absence of a patent, and that immunity carried with it the forms, even in the case of one who sold them for use by others.

"Explanation" was thus set apart from use at least where the copyrighted work taught a practical art. Denial of copyright to commonplace advertisements[87] and to such ephemeral fact collections as market quotations[88]—settled doctrine before 1909—was justified on grounds of their being works merely of utility; it was also suggested that they did not meet the constitutional standard of promoting science or arts. So also the substance of news reports was conceived to be free of copyright, though special literary style or embellishment

[86]101 U.S. 99 (1879).
[87]J. L. Mott Iron Works v. Clow, 82 Fed. 316 (7th Cir. 1897).
[88]Clayton v. Stone, 5 Fed. Cas. 999 (No. 2872) (C.C.S.D.N.Y. 1829).

might perhaps claim protection.[89] But what of the protection of compilations, directories, and the like which assembled facts? Discussing news carried by ticker tape, Judge Grosscup, in a case anticipating the great quarrel between Associated Press and International News Service,[90] offered a distinction between "originality" and "opportunity," between works of authorship and mere annals;[91] but one may wonder whether it was really fair to say that compilations were works of the creative mind while news reports sprang just from occasion.

The 350 years of this lecture, from the stationers' charter of 1557 to the threshold of our act of 1909, end, fittingly enough, with some attempts at generalization by Justice Holmes. *Bleistein v. Donaldson Lithographing Co.*[92] upheld the copyrightability of three humble chromolithographs picturing certain circus acts as advertisements of Wallace's circus. On principle, Holmes thought, any work qualified for copyright so far as it was a "personal reaction . . . upon nature." "Personality always contains something unique. It expresses its singularity even in handwriting, and a very modest grade of art has in it something irreducible, which is one man's alone. That something he may copyright unless there is a restriction in the words of the act." The pictures were not barred on account of their "limited pretensions": "the least pretentious picture has more originality in it than directories and the like." Nor did it matter that the pictures advertised goods or services.

[89] See Tribune Co. of Chicago v. Associated Press, 116 Fed. 126 (C.C.N.D. Ill. 1900); BOWKER, COPYRIGHT: ITS HISTORY AND ITS LAW 89 (1912).
[90] See *infra,* Lecture III, pp. 86-87.
[91] National Tel. News Co. v. Western Union Tel. Co., 119 Fed. 294, 298 (7th Cir. 1902).
[92] 188 U.S. 239 (1903).

The opinion upset brusquely the received wisdom about advertising matter. But more arresting was Holmes's insistence on individuality or personality which seems to me to have an echo in it of the Romantic gospel.[93]

Assume a copyright in some manifestation of individuality —just what restraint did it work on others? The Court held in *White-Smith Music Pub. Co. v. Apollo Co.*[94] that the copyright of a song was not infringed by the manufacture and sale of music rolls which, when used on player pianos, rendered the music in sound. Although agreeing that the matter was concluded by precedent, Holmes objected on principle. The ground of copyright was that the author had "invented some new collocation of visible or audible points." Protection should not extend beyond "the specific form, . . . the collocation devised"; on the other hand the protection should go to the "essence" of the collocation; it ought to be "coextensive not only with the invention, which, though free to all, only one had the ability to achieve, but with the possibility of reproducing the result which gives to the invention its meaning and worth." Holmes's language here leaves some doubt as to what he meant by "invention." Also, is protection of "the specific form" of the invention, the same thing as protecting its "result"? The latter might be read as taking in a good deal more than the former. Thus we come to *Kalem Co. v. Harper Bros.*,[95] where the defendant had made a silent

[93]*Cf.* Warren & Brandeis, *The Right to Privacy*, 4 Harv. L. Rev. 193, 205 (1890), relating the right of the sender of a letter to prevent its publication, and indeed all rights to prevent publication of "thoughts, sentiments, and emotions, expressed through the medium of writings or of the arts" to "the more general right of the individual to be let alone."
[94]209 U.S. 1 (1908) (Justice Holmes "concurring specially" at 18).
[95]222 U.S. 55 (1911).

motion picture following the story of the copyrighted novel
Ben Hur. Had not the "form" of the novel been changed,
and even the "result"? Here was an opportunity to descant
on plagiarism but Holmes dealt with the problem briefly.
Although the statute said nothing about movies until 1912,
it had already prohibited "dramatization," and a movie was
not less a drama than a faithful pantomime would be, and
hence should count as a dramatization of the novel. To the
claim that expansion of the copyright of the novel to prohibit
the movie would create a monopoly of "ideas" in violation of
the copyright clause of the Constitution, Holmes answered
that the law had not that effect but "confines itself to a
particular, cognate and well known form of reproduction";
and he ended characteristically, "If to that extent a grant of
monopoly is thought a proper way to secure the right to the
writings this court cannot say that Congress was wrong." We
get no view of how far Holmes would have been willing to
suppress the individuality of a movie producer who did not
so much follow *Ben Hur* as ring variations on it, just as the
movie varied from the protectible part of the play in *Sheldon
v. Metro-Goldwyn Pictures Corp.*—the case with which we
began, and to which we must return in the next lecture.

I have rendered a summary of the evolution of Anglo-
American doctrine about copyright, of the gradual broaden-
ing of that conception; and instead of summarizing the sum-
mary I shall recall the main protagonists of the tale: John
Doe, unknown draftsman of the Stationers' Company charter;
Archbishop Whitgift, probable author of the Star Chamber
decree of 1586; Richard Roe, draftsman of the Statute of
Anne; Lord Mansfield, associated with the classic narrow

view of the horizontal extent of copyright; Edward Young, arbitrarily chosen as the voice of Romanticism; Lord Eldon, transitional figure; Justice Story, American expositor; and, finally, Justice Holmes.

II. Plagiarism Reexamined*

THE FIRST lecture, attempting to explain how copyright spun wider its ancient web, brought us to about 1909, with the law still inchoate. Now I must try to give you a sketch of the notional shape of copyright after another half-century's development, and for that purpose I shall pursue, mainly, the subjects of copyrightability and infringement which are close, almost Siamese, partners. To vary the figure, I shall take you on a stroll over some of the copyright terrain and examine various knolls and gullies in a rather desultory, even naïve way; finally we shall climb to the top of a hill and see whether anything can be usefully said about the whole landscape.

But first we need to say a word about our statute of 1909, which, with emendations, is still in force.[1] It is a peculiarly busy piece of legislation crammed with details on matters ranging from the formalities of notice, registration, and so forth, through the renewal mechanics, remedies, and requirement of domestic manufacture, to a compulsory license for

*The title is somewhat a misnomer since I touch also on piracy, and on infringement generally. "In piracy, unlicensed persons still give the author credit; in plagiarism they take the credit themselves." Chafee, *Reflections on the Law of Copyright: I*, 45 COLUM. L. REV. 503, 513 (1945).

[1]The statute in its present form is codified as Title 17, United States Code (1964).

mechanical reproductions of music (a response to the *White-Smith* music-roll problem on which Holmes had written in 1908[2]). On the more basic themes: the statute first describes the subject matter of copyright as including "all the writings of an author,"[3] which seemingly covers all of Holmes's "collocations" and perhaps goes further and exhausts any larger content the constitutional clause may have. There follows in the statute, however, an enumeration of categories of works[4] which can be and as a practical matter has been read to limit the general statement.[5] The categories listed do not seem to encompass measurably more than previous legislation, but that had already taken in an extensive subject matter. "Newspapers" are now mentioned,[6] but "books" had already comprehended written material in various forms, and the reference to newspapers does not itself decide whether news as such can now claim protection. The category "works of art" appears without the limiting word "fine,"[7] but Holmes had disposed of that qualifier in his *Bleistein* opinion on the chromolithographic advertisements.[8] Then as to rights in copyrightable subject matter, the act, besides vesting the broad rights to "print, reprint, publish, copy, and vend," proceeds in prolix style to spell out rights appropriate to given categories of works, such as the right to perform or represent.[9] Apart from

[2]*Supra* p. 35.
[3]17 U.S.C. § 4.
[4]17 U.S.C. § 5 (actually a classification of works for purposes of registration).
[5]See Mazer v. Stein, 347 U.S. 201, 210-11 & nn. 17-19 (1954); Capitol Records, Inc. v. Mercury Records Corp., 221 F.2d 657, 661 (2d Cir. 1955).
[6]17 U.S.C. § 5(b)
[7]17 U.S.C. § 5(g).
[8]*Supra* p. 34.
[9]17 U.S.C. § 1.

certain distinct limits, such as the confinement of the drama-performance right to public performance,[10] and the music-performance right to public performance for profit,[11] the rights vested in the proprietor are expressed in blanket form—in the style of an "exclusive right" in such-and-such a way to replicate the work. Left at large, then, are the questions: what elements of a work are protected against the replication?, what takings are actionable? We can, however, say that the draftsmen, following uncomplainingly the desires of copyright proprietors, wanted the monopoly to extend somehow to various transformations of, or derivatives from, copyrighted works: in addition to translation and dramatization,[12] the statute now mentions novelization, adaptation, arrangement, "other versions,"[13] and—in a curiously ambiguous or left-handed way—abridgment.[14] I should mention, finally, that while the initial term of copyright remains twenty-eight years, as set by the act of 1831,[15] the renewal term is lengthened from fourteen to twenty-eight years.[16]

I do not mean to reproach the draftsmen for failing to face squarely the questions of validity and infringement which are in the end insoluble. Rather I make the point that the statute, like its predecessors, leaves the development of fundamentals to the judges. Indeed the courts have had to be consulted at nearly every point, for the text of the statute has a maddeningly casual prolixity and imprecision throughout. One takes

[10]17 U.S.C. § 1(d).
[11]17 U.S.C. § 1(e).
[12]17 U.S.C. § 1(b).
[13]*Ibid.*
[14]17 U.S.C. § 7.
[15]Act of 3 February 1831, ch. 16, § 1, 4 Stat. 436.
[16]17 U.S.C. § 24.

1909 as a starting place not merely because of the fact of recodification, but because there was thenceforth a crowding of suggestive case law. My concern is now less historical and more analytic, but a certain continuity is provided through the fact that Judge Learned Hand (who was appointed to the bench in the same year 1909) contributed greatly to the ventilation of copyright doctrine[17] and in this lecture is seen as the chief actor.

One of Judge Hand's earliest copyright cases plunged him into the problem—not solved but rather renewed by Holmes's references to both "personality" and "invention"[18]—whether, in respect to validity and infringement, copyright was to sail under the flag of patent or under its own strange device. In *Hein v. Harris*,[19] Judge Hand held the defendant's song "I Think I Hear a Woodpecker Knocking at My Family Tree" to be an infringement of the plaintiff's "Arab Love Song" over the defendant's protestation that he had never known the plaintiff's work. This lack of copying Judge Hand thought immaterial; enough that the defendant's song was composed later than the plaintiff's and was similar to it. The defendant had also urged as a defense that the plaintiff's song closely resembled others extant when the plaintiff wrote. Judge Hand was not very clear about the pertinence of the prior art, but spoke of the plaintiff's work as being a sufficient "invention" though in style similar to earlier melodies, which hints that a

[17]*Cf.* Cracas, *Judge Learned Hand and the Law of Copyright*, in 7 ASCAP, Copyright Law Symposium 55 (1956).
[18]*Supra* p. 35.
[19]175 Fed. 875 (C.C.S.D.N.Y. 1910), *aff'd*, 183 Fed. 107 (2d Cir. 1910); see also Judge Hand's opinion in Stodart v. Mutual Film Corp., 249 Fed. 507 (S.D.N.Y. 1917), *aff'd*, 249 Fed. 513 (2d Cir. 1918).

copyright could be invalidated by mere anticipation. Thus copyright was seemingly assimilated to patent.

In 1924 Judge Hand retreated from this position. *Fred Fisher, Inc. v. Dillingham*[20] held that Jerome Kern, ingenious composer though he was, had committed a plagiarism: a part—a small part, to be sure—of his song "Kalua" infringed Bernard's "Dardanella." Kern's ostinato or repeated figure used as an accompaniment to his chorus was much the same as Bernard's ostinato accompanying the verse. Kern swore he was unconscious of having taken from "Dardanella," and Judge Hand believed him. That would be irrelevant under Hand's previous view. It remained irrelevant, but now under a quite different view. Judge Hand now thought there could be no infringement without copying from the plaintiff's work. He concluded, however, that the plaintiff's work was actually the source of the defendant's: the defendant had copied though without conscious intention; he knew "Dardanella" very well as a hit song, and his memory must have played him a trick. But could the plaintiff hold a copyright when, as the proof showed, his figure had been anticipated by an adaptation of Weber's "Mermaid Song" by one Landon? That did not matter in the absence of proof that the plaintiff had copied from Landon. This rule as to validity was correlative with the rule on infringement. Both questions turned on originality, that is, spontaneity or absence of copying, a psychological matter; they did not turn on invention, the production of something that did not exist in the prior art, an historical matter.

Judge Hand argued that unless originality was the test,

[20]298 Fed. 145 (S.D.N.Y. 1924).

works such as compilations could rarely claim copyright. This
consideration alone is perhaps not convincing. It is not self-
evident that a rule fitting works of industrious collection must
also be applied to works of imagination; indeed even a test of
originality can hardly be applied in the same sense to both
classes. And while innocence of copying makes a strong
appeal, considered as a defense to a charge of infringement,
it has less appeal, when offered as the foundation of an
affirmative claim of protection. So the correlation is not as
obvious as Hand supposed. But novelty would in all events be
a poor criterion. If it is a difficult, perhaps an illusory, measure
in the field of mechanical improvements, how much harder
would it be in literature or the other arts. Starting even with
the bias of an extreme Romanticism, how does one determine
what is "new," or significantly or importantly new? And is it
newness, a fresh departure from the past, that we want
uniquely to encourage by law? In time a standard of novelty
would have to be debased or distorted, else copyright as a
system would lose all viability. The idea that the tonal scale
is finite perhaps had momentarily misled Hand into thinking
that an analysis in terms of novelty could be applied feasibly
to musical compositions.[21]

But was originality a permissible criterion of copyright
under the "author" part of the constitutional clause? Judge
Frank showed in the *Alfred Bell* case[22] that it was—although
perhaps not the only criterion that Congress could elect to

[21]In Arnstein v. Edward B. Marks Music Corp., 82 F.2d 275 (2d Cir.
1936), Judge Hand wrote for the Circuit Court of Appeals adopting the
view of Fred Fisher, Inc. v. Dillingham and overturning Hein v. Harris,
supra note 19.

[22]Alfred Bell & Co., Ltd. v. Catalda Fine Arts, Inc., 191 F.2d 99 (2d Cir.
1951).

use. With the originality concept correctly installed as central, copyright appeared as relatively easy to achieve but as correspondingly modest in its pretensions to monopoly. This apparent modesty of the system attracts sympathy, and we find Judge Hand later suggesting to an incredulous patent bar that they make over patent on the model of copyright.[23]

What the prior art consists of remains significant, however, even when originality calls the turn in copyright. The defendant in an infringement action may have a hard job establishing by definite proof that the plaintiff resorted to prior works, and was thus a copyist not an author, even when there is a good natural chance that he did so because similar works abounded. But if that was the condition of the prior art, the defendant may well be believed when he undertakes to show that he took from that store, and not from the plaintiff—his "disclaimer becomes more plausible."[24] Indeed the courts will sometimes hold simply on a footing of common sense, without precise proof, that the plaintiff must have leaned whether consciously or not on the preexisting material. This can of course be more readily done where the alleged plagiarism is claimed to lie in the imitation of a "pattern" in the plaintiff's work rather than in delineated details. But we must note that if imputations of knowledge of the prior art were made too lightly, novelty would tend to be reinstated as a requirement of holding a copyright.

[23]*Hearings, "American Patent System," October 10-12, 1955, Subcommittee on Patents, Trademarks, and Copyrights of the Senate Committee on the Judiciary*, 84th Cong., 1st Sess., at 114 (1956).

[24]Sheldon v. Metro-Goldwyn Pictures Corp., 81 F.2d 49, 54 (2d Cir.), *cert. denied*, 298 U.S. 669 (1936); Detective Comics, Inc. v. Bruns Pub., Inc., 111 F.2d 432, 433 (2d Cir. 1940).

Are there compositions which though original are too small to qualify for copyright or to figure as the subjects of actionable infringement? Some of Holmes's language suggests that any emanation of personality, however slight, any uncopied collocation, however slim, should be protected, and his abnegation of judicial responsibility for passing on the merit of intellectual productions points in the same direction.[25] So also does the appearance in the statute of so mean a category as "prints or labels used for articles of merchandise"[26]—though we must always beware of a false development of copyright law by a process of treating extreme applications as being normal, thus inviting applications even more extreme.[27] There are, on the other hand, definite indications of some rule *de minimis*.

Some have thought it inherent in the very notion of "personality," of spontaneity, that a copyright claimant must exceed the utterly stilted or trite, must satisfy some threshold requirement of "creativity."[28] And though Judge Frank pushed hard in the *Alfred Bell* case to show the theoretical protectibility of any original production, he still admitted that a variation, say, on a public domain work must be more than "trivial" to support copyright.[29] Judge Hand wrote to similar

[25]See Bleistein v. Donaldson Lithographing Co., 188 U.S. 239 (1903), quoted from *supra* p. 34.

[26]17 U.S.C. § 5(k).

[27]*Cf.* Lord Robertson's remarks, dissenting in Walter v. Lane, [1900] A.C. 539, 561.

[28]See REGISTER OF COPYRIGHTS, COPYRIGHT LAW REVISION: REPORT ON THE GENERAL REVISION OF THE U.S. COPYRIGHT LAW, printed for the use of the House Comm. on the Judiciary, 87th Cong., 1st Sess., at 9 (Comm. Print 1961). *But see* SUPPLEMENTARY REPORT, COPYRIGHT LAW REVISION, PT. 6, at 3 (Comm. Print 1965) (89th Cong., 1st Sess.), where an express requirement of "creativity" is abandoned.

[29]Alfred Bell & Co., Ltd. v. Catalda Fine Arts, Inc., 191 F.2d 99, 103 (2d Cir. 1951).

effect in the *National Comics* case.[30] Courts are disinclined
to permit copyright to attach to short word sequences or to find
plagiarism in the copying of such sequences; this lies close
to the slogan that "titles" are not protected through copyright.[31]
More generally it has been said that only substantial takings
are actionable: Judge Hand would apply this to the appropriation of a separate scene or part of the dialogue of a play,
and thought the same question of substantiality arose in
adjudging infringement of any work.[32] We can, I think, conclude that to make the copyright turnstile revolve, the author
should have to deposit more than a penny in the box, and
some like measure ought to apply to infringement. Surely
there is danger in trying to fence off small quanta of words
or other collocations; these pass quickly into the idiom; to
allow them copyright, particularly if aided by a doctrine of
"unconscious" plagiarism, could set up untoward barriers to
expression. But in this light we can question the soundness of
a number of modern decisions and may, indeed, start by asking
whether Judge Hand was right to protect the phrase in the
song "Dardanella."

The case of *Abie's Irish Rose—Nichols v. Universal Pictures
Corp.*[33]—takes us to the opposite end of the scale and reassures
us, notwithstanding the fears I expressed in the first lecture
about the erasure of any line between "idea" and "form" or

[30]National Comics Pub., Inc. v. Fawcett Pub., Inc., 191 F.2d 594, 600
(2d Cir. 1951).
[31]*Cf.* Regulations of the Copyright Office, 37 C.F.R., ch. II, § 202.1(a)
(1959). See also NIMMER, COPYRIGHT § 34 (1965). *But cf.* Heim v. Universal Pictures Co., Inc., 154 F.2d 480, 487 n. 8 (2d Cir. 1946); Life Music,
Inc. v. Wonderland Music Co., 241 F. Supp. 653, 656 (S.D.N.Y. 1965).
[32]Nichols v. Universal Pictures Corp., 45 F.2d 119, 121 (2d Cir. 1930),
cert. denied, 282 U.S. 902 (1931).
[33]*Supra* note 2

"expression," that there are still some patterns too big for copyright protection. Resting on the doctrine growing out of *Daly v. Palmer*, the case of the railroad rescue scene,[34] Ann Nichols charged infringement of her play by the movie *The Cohens and the Kellys*, in that the defendant had taken the complex of her plot and characters. The defendant had not lifted any of Nichols's dialogue. Judge Hand declined, although he was apparently tempted, to dismiss the action on a common-sense judgment that as to those aspects of Nichols's simpleminded play of which the defendant could be found a copyist, Nichols must herself have drawn from the previous literature, rife with confrontations between Jews and Irishmen. On the contrary, Judge Hand scrupulously assumed that Nichols's play was original and that the defendant had copied from the play. The controlling point was that on comparison of the play with the movie it appeared that the defendant had taken, at most, Nichols's "ideas" not her "expression": the plot at a generalized level, the characters only as general types. These "ideas" the plaintiff's copyright could not cover, for so to "generalize" her copyright would tend to bar subsequent writers from too large a precinct. It may be suggested that the offense to the public interest involved in permitting such a generalization of copyright would be not less but more serious, had there been startling innovation in the ideas of Miss Nichols's work, for then it would be all the more important to allow others to manipulate the ideas freely.

In explanation of how he reached the *Nichols* result, Judge

[34] 6 Fed. Cas. 1132 (No. 3552) (C.C.S.D.N.Y. 1868), discussed *supra* p. 31.

Hand said in that case: "Upon any work, and especially upon a play, a great number of patterns of increasing generality will fit equally well, as more and more of the incident is left out." We are to find "the most detailed pattern, common to both" the accusing and the accused works.[35] Does that pattern comprehend only "ideas" or "ideas" together with "expression"? If the latter, then there is infringement to the extent of the "expression" except as some other factor may excuse. Somewhere in the process, when applied to plays, we are to take account of the "characters" besides the incidents, for both in combination are, according to Judge Hand, the "substance."[36]

Hand's explanation does, I think, sharpen our awareness of what we are about, but surely the technique described lacks precision. We are in a viscid quandary once we admit that "expression" can consist of anything not close aboard the particular collocation in its sequential order. The job of comparison is not much eased by speaking of patterns, nor is the task of deciding when the monopoly would be too broad for the public convenience made much neater by speaking of ideas and expression. The polarity proposed by Hand is indeed related geneologically to the ancient opposition of idea to form, but the ancestor is not readily recognized in the ambiguous and elusive descendant.

I return to the *Sheldon* case,[37] the starting point of the first lecture, which on any view is harder than *Nichols*. Judge

---

[35]45 F.2d at 121.
[36]*Ibid.*
[37]Sheldon v. Metro-Goldwyn Pictures Corp., 81 F.2d 49 (2d Cir.), *cert. denied*, 298 U.S. 669 (1936).

Hand's opinion in *Sheldon* is a virtuoso piece of writing.[38] Four similar stories—Madeleine Smith's, the play, the novel, the picture—are told and compared, yet there is no impression of wearisome repetition. Criticism is disarmed until one reads the record and examines carefully Judge Woolsey's opinion below holding for the defendants.[39]

Judge Woolsey was not as much committed to the pattern analysis as was Judge Hand; yet their techniques were not markedly at variance. But one quickly sees how formulation of the common pattern of greatest specificity can be decisively altered by shifts of emphasis that come in almost imperceptibly; and what is to count as a detail or a larger structure is similarly biased. In fact we do not get from Hand, still less from Woolsey, an articulated statement of what the common pattern was—from which there would have to be subtracted, as it were, those elements of the motion picture as to which the plaintiffs could not claim authorship or charge plagiarism (that is, the elements deriving from the true story or the Lowndes novel). Had the whole operation been literally carried out, it might appear that there were few similarities that could figure as unexcused imitations of "expression," and those so discrete and of such a dimension as to be nonactionable. I would suggest, too, that the repeated avowal that copyrighted material is not exempt from use, only from copying in detail, ought to mean, at least as regards imaginative works, that even details can be used, and recognizably so, if they are "improved" by changes in which the user himself displays substantial

[38]Here I am in happy agreement with George Wharton Pepper, who expressed his admiration for the opinion in *The Literary Style of Learned Hand*, 60 HARV. L. REV. 333, 340-41 (1947).

[39]7 F. Supp. 837 (S.D.N.Y. 1934).

authorship. Here I take inspiration from Lord Mansfield's thinking.[40] I cannot escape a feeling that Hand was influenced by the evidence that the defendants had consciously tried to run as close as they thought they safely could to the design of the play.[41] I think Hand also allowed himself some dubious judgments about which turns of plot or aspects of character were peculiarly important in making the play highly actable and accounting for its success.

The infringing "expression" found in the *Sheldon* case comprised not only some of the features of the plot but also some lineaments of the characters. In the *Nichols* case Judge Hand had considered *obiter* whether, separately from the plots, a character in one play could be copied into a character in another play to the point of infringement. He said: "If *Twelfth Night* were copyrighted, it is quite possible that a second comer might so closely imitate Sir Toby Belch or Malvolio as to infringe, but it would not be enough that for one of his characters he cast a riotous knight who kept wassail to the discomfort of his household, or a vain and foppish steward who became amorous of his mistress. These would be no more than Shakespeare's 'ideas' in the play. . . . It follows that the less developed the characters, the less they can be copyrighted; that is the penalty an author must bear for marking them too indistinctly."[42] (We must assume for this example that the second comer did not suggest, say by calling his characters by their original names, that his work was written by Shakespeare: that would add extraneous problems of "passing off.")

[40]See also Clark, C.J., in MacDonald v. DuMaurier, 144 F.2d 696, 702 (2d Cir. 1944) (dissenting opinion).
[41]*Cf.* Davis v. E. I. du Pont de Nemours & Co., 240 F. Supp. 612 (S.D. N.Y. 1965), which in several respects is reminiscent of the Sheldon case.
[42]45 F.2d at 121.

Now I should have thought that literary characters, in plays as in novels, achieve their distinctness in large part by being made to react to the particular flux of incident in the particular milieu. Consider how Malvolio is to be described free of the complex of *Twelfth Night*. As Malvolio's analogue (with a different name) was moved through different surroundings and episodes, the pattern common to both characters would tend to describe only a stock figure, "idea" not "expression," unless the latter term is held to cover far too much. Thus there is not a little trouble in extricating "character" as a separately copyrightable element; and I imagine there would be like difficulty with other features such as setting—features which some specialists have perhaps too easily treated as "extricable."[43] I think no case of infringement of a literary character independent of plot has yet arisen.[44] Such infringement may be more plausibly claimed as between pictorial characters. But in the *Detective Comics* case[45] in the Second Circuit, in which, at the suit of the cartoon character "Superman," an injunction went against a "Wonderman" similarly girt, the further likeness in plots or incidents seems to have been a ponderable factor in the finding of infringement. In a later case where "Superman" accused another imitator, "Captain Marvel," Judge Hand read the *Detective*

[43]See Wincor, *The Seven Basic Program Properties,* 47 TRADEMARK REP. 440-41 (1957). See also WINCOR, FROM RITUAL TO ROYALTIES (1962), ch. 3.

[44]The Maltese Falcon Case, Warner Bros. Pictures, Inc. v. Columbia Broadcasting System, Inc., 216 F.2d 945 (9th Cir. 1954), *cert. denied,* 348 U.S. 971 (1955), is wide of the present mark, and some of its observations on the question of "characters" are surely wrong. See Kaplan, Book Review, 78 HARV. L. REV. 1094, 1097 (1965).

[45]Detective Comics, Inc. v. Bruns Pub., Inc., 111 F.2d 432 (2d Cir. 1940).

Comics case quite restrictively and tied "Captain Marvel's" infringement to the lifting of specific exploits.[46] The problem is a teasing one. In a visual way cartoon characters appear delineated, but in other respects they are usually stock characters to the ultimate degree. Hence there is bound to be trouble in setting proper bounds to their protection.

Judge Hand first applied his pattern technique to ordinary plays where the chief or only interest lay in the unfolding of action through characters: this interest provided the spindle or axis for the successive patterns, and the patterns could be expressed as ordinary narratives. I suggest that the process is harder when applied to conventional novels, and the results less telling, since the materials of such works are more diffuse. Where "representational" elements are subordinated or absent —the so-called antinovels and antiplays would furnish extreme examples—I suggest that the eduction of patterns would be an exceedingly slippery business and in the end futile. Courts of the present day ought to find infringement here only in fairly specific tracking; that might serve a higher purpose in permitting a large freedom of literary experimentation. Nonfanciful scholarly works on the style of treatises, on the other hand, lend themselves readily to patterning according to their "arguments" (to use the old-fashioned word), but in many cases the possibilities of feasible variation are limited.[47] This must influence the place where the line should be fixed between "idea" and "expression" in the most detailed common web.

[46]National Comics Pub., Inc. v. Fawcett Pub., Inc., 191 F.2d 594, 600 (2d Cir. 1951).
[47]See Justice Story's opinion in Emerson v. Davies, 8 Fed. Cas. 615, 624 (No. 4436) (C.C.D.Mass. 1845).

Is it useful to try to apply "idea," "expression," "patterns" to musical copyright? In several cases involving popular music, Judge Hand seems to have regarded melody as the crux and to have paid little attention to other elements such as harmony.[48] Such emphasis on the succession of tones might offend against the view that for a finding of infringement of popular music, the average innocent ear must perceive substantial similarity, for other elements of the composition besides melody may influence that perception. In any event, how are we to answer the question whether a simple, indeed any, melodic line is not more properly classified as "idea" than as "expression"?[49] Unless we are to scout all possibility of infringement, we are again remitted to close and sustained parallelism as a basis for liability. As to "serious" music, the axes of possible interest, as I have called them, become more numerous and patterning unsure. The musical tradition tolerates considerable definite and deliberate borrowing provided the later composer manipulates what he has taken. This may be the point of the tale about the composer who, treating the Ten Commandments a a musical subject, unabashedly took a generous helping from someone else's work when he came to the Commandment "Thou shalt not steal." Having in mind the nature of the audience, the proclivities of music critics, the unlikelihood that borrowing diverts profit from the original composer, we may agree that the law can afford to take a permissive attitude toward cross-lifting among serious musical works.

[48] See SHAFTER, MUSICAL COPYRIGHT 204-05 (2d ed. 1939).
[49] See Sawer, *Some Problems in the Law of Copyright*, 4 RES JUDICATAE 155-56 (1950). *Cf.* L. Hand, D.J., in Reiss v. National Quotation Bureau, Inc., 276 Fed. 717, 718 (S.D.N.Y. 1921): "Music is not normally a representative art. . . ."

The apparatus of the *Nichols* and *Sheldon* cases offers but weak guides for settling the plethora of current disputes over graphic works. Here a short preface is needed. There was doubt prior to the Supreme Court decision of *Mazer v. Stein*[50] in 1954 whether designs or other graphic productions which might themselves qualify as "works of art" could claim copyright as applied to, or embodied in, utilitarian goods (or could be infringed by being duplicated on, or in the form of, such goods). There was first the problem of "utility" which appeared in a couple of guises in the previous lecture. Second, for a long time we have had on the books a statute allowing patent for ornamental designs of articles of manufacture.[51] It seems a foolish statute for insisting on invention, a chimerical requirement for artistic works. Be that as it may, the statute might be thought the only shelter for the cases supposed and to preclude alternative or accumulative protection by way of copyright. In the *Mazer* case, however, the Supreme Court opened the door to copyright—no one knows just how far—and there has been a parade of infringement actions based on fancy lamp bases, on designs for cloth, on junk jewelry, on dolls, on artificial flowers, on inflatable plastic Santa Clauses, *inter alia enormia.* Judge Hand frankly said in the *Peter Pan* case involving a design imprinted on dress goods, "In the case of designs, which are addressed to the aesthetic sensibilities of an observer, the test"—of idea, expression, and so forth—"is, if possible, even more intangible."[52] The case is like that of music for which the "test" is very infirm. But we need to go

[50]347 U.S. 201 (1954).
[51]35 U.S.C. § 171 (1964).
[52]Peter Pan Fabrics, Inc. v. Martin Weiner Corp., 274 F.2d 487, 489 (2d Cir. 1960).

further and consider the several natures of the varieties of goods within the possible reach of the *Mazer* doctrine, and the markets in which they appear. Copyright itself seems out of place where the artistic structure is only one of a number of elements attracting customers to the particular goods, that is, where the goods are not "fragile" in the sense in which books customarily are. What power, moreover, do we want to give to a seller by means of the copyright to threaten to block entry into a field? Think here of cases where all sellers must bring their designs within the perimeter of a seasonal fashion that sets a limit on feasible variation. Full analysis would, I think, tend to justify a copyright, if at all, only when the artistic component is primary; even then the copyright should serve to prevent only close imitation. I think some cases following *Mazer,* including, possibly, the *Peter Pan* case itself, have granted protection pretty loosely, and I would join in Judge Clark's protest, dissenting in the *Ideal Toy* case,[53] against the unthinking acceptance of strained claims of illicit copying. It is an apprehension, perhaps subliminal, of the dangers of injecting copyright into complex, going market mechanisms rather than any indication of precise limits in the *Mazer* opinion itself that accounts for the general acceptance of the proposition that the configuration of dresses, hats, and other articles of apparel cannot hold copyright at all under the present law.[54] The bills introduced in Congress over the past several years which would extend the régime of copyright to the apparel field, and beyond that to a vague field of

[53]Ideal Toy Corp. v. Sayco Doll Corp., 302 F.2d 623, 626-27 (2d Cir. 1962).

[54]See Regulations of the Copyright Office, 37 C.F.R., ch. II, § 202.10 (1959).

"industrial" designs,[55] seem to me a curious form of super-erogative folly.

Passing from infringement of works of some "utility" to imitation of works of "fine art" (if I may resurrect that expression), Judge Hand's deprecation of the "test" would be all the more just. Here the manner of execution is usually of more interest than the subject pictured. If standard works like David's *Rape of the Sabines*, which Picasso recently chose to redo, were under copyright, not only would Picasso fail to infringe, he would, I think, be nearly incapable of doing so even if he put his mind to it.

The *Nichols* and *Sheldon* opinions barely noted that the offending works were not plays, as were the originals, but movies. So inured have we become to the extension of the monopoly to a large range of so-called derivative works, that we no longer sense the oddity of accepting such an enlargement of copyright while yet intoning the abacadabra of "idea" and "expression." Change of medium is nevertheless an interesting and sometimes baffling variable to be added to the infringement calculus. I suppose paintings inspired by copyrighted music, music inspired by copyrighted paintings, would be thought noninfringing. It is not a breach of the

---

[55]A "design protection" bill was passed by the Senate in the 87th, and again in the 88th Congress (S. 1884, S. 776). Very recently, on 27 July 1966, the Senate passed S. 1237, 89th Cong., 2d Sess., another such bill, which, however, would exempt designs "composed of three-dimensional features of shape and surface with respect to men's, women's, and children's apparel, including undergarments and outerwear." See S. Rep. No. 1404, 89th Cong., 2d Sess., at 4, noting that the opposition of the Justice Department is based in part on reservations about the constitutional reach of the copyright power with regard to ornamental designs of useful articles. On that point, see Douglas, J., in Mazer v. Stein, 347 U.S. 201, 219-21 (1954).

copyright of a poem to try to capture its essence in glass sculpture, as artists in that medium recently sought to do. This would be about as free of legal consequences as Hemingway's allegation that he copied his writing style from Cézanne's paintings. Getting to more plausible cases, while a motion picture may be a mere replica of a copyrighted play, and thereby infringe, plays commonly are much altered, and novels even more so, as they are transmuted into motion pictures. It is often thought necessary to make drastic changes of dialogue, action, and other elements in order to keep the picture faithful to the original. But if it is a matter of nice artistic judgment how much change is needed to attain "sameness" in the new medium, we can anticipate difficulties in deciding what is infringement. It is surely wrong to assume that what Hollywood is content to call a dramatization or screen treatment of a novel or play would necessarily be an infringing copy if not licensed. The fundamental that "use" is not the same thing as "infringement," that use short of infringement is to be encouraged, is relevant to these transformation cases. Again I think it is relevant in considering how far the copyrights of the James Bond series or *Mary Poppins* can be permitted to assure a right to exclude the vast array of works and products that can be conjured up to recall the originals: the more remote are in the nature of mere commentaries on publicized facts. "Passing off" theory is naturally invoked when the copyright theory seems thin, but will often be found a pretense, the public being neither concerned nor confused about source. A use of a copyrighted work may amount to "parasitism" and still be permissible. Thus a man does not infringe if in some spirit of parody he publishes new words which the reader is encouraged to sing to the music of a song copyrighted by another both as to the music and the original words.[56] Here we have a kind of pickaback ride on the copyright, but I think it is properly held to be a permissible ride.[57]

Let us move from works of imagination or intellect to "fact works," first noting that the categories cannot be tidily set apart. Judge Hand said that fact collections might initially have been put outside the range of copyright law, for here "form" (or "expression") is unimportant.[58] I noted earlier that "originality" does not quite fit, either. But the copyright statutes extended protection to "books" all-inclusively; an exception for fact works would have been intrinsically hard to maintain; and there was no other body of doctrine to which such works could have made an easy appeal for protection. They still have an uncomfortable perch in the copyright law. Their functional peculiarities have received some, but still not enough open recognition by the courts; even Judge Hand, like Justice Holmes before him, on occasion reasoned from these works to works of imagination.[59]

Professor Gorman has written thoughtfully of fact works

[56] Berlin v. E. C. Publications, Inc., 329 F.2d 541 (2d Cir.), *cert. denied,* 379 U.S. 822 (1964).

[57] I would question the analysis in Addison-Wesley Pub. Co. v. Brown, 223 F. Supp. 219 (E.D.N.Y. 1963) (answer-book infringes copyrighted physics course book). See also the same case on preliminary injunction, 207 F. Supp. 678 (E.D.N.Y. 1962).

[58] Jewelers' Circ. Pub. Co. v. Keystone Pub. Co., 274 Fed. 932, 935 (S.D. N.Y. 1921), *aff'd,* 281 Fed. 83 (2d Cir.), *cert. denied,* 259 U.S. 581 (1922).

[59] See Hand's reasoning in rejecting "novelty" as the basis of copyright, *supra* pp. 42-43; and Holmes's reasoning in relating copyright to a manifestation of personality, *supra* p. 34.

and I shall not go over the whole ground.[60] Take as an archetype a directory collecting humdrum information, the result of labor in physically gathering and then in presenting the facts. It is now pretty clear that a later publisher must expend some of the same kind of investigative effort to avoid infringement. But there are questions, never resolved in this country and probably beyond resolution, about just how far the first work, though unavailable as a mere template for copying, can be referred to and used as a check upon, or as an incidental aid to, the later production.[61] It would be a waste of effort and time as well as a practical impossibility to require of a collector complete abnegation of past collections. Such abnegation as is demanded serves a purpose in forcing a re-canvass, thus promoting accuracy or currency on the part of the later worker, but the adjustments attained in the decisions have not been nicely calibrated to the policy.[62] I am reminded of dictionaries which are not at too far a remove from direc-tories: I would think it a trying assignment to have to prepare cautionary instructions for lexicographers, starting out to write a new dictionary, as to the extent to which they could consult dictionaries already in copyright (which in turn of course relied on older dictionaries). The whole problem will certainly be renewed in a most acute way in relation to the manipula-tion of data collections by the new breed of electronic devices.

Consider, next, published news accounts either in staccato or elaborated prose. What may another publisher take without

---

[60]Gorman, *Copyright Protection for the Collection and Representation of Facts*, 76 Harv. L. Rev. 1569 (1963).

[61]See L. Hand, D.J., in the Jewelers' Circular case, *supra* note 58, 274 Fed. at 935.

[62]Gorman, *supra* note 60, at 1570.

infringing? The rule of the *I.N.S.* case[63] condemns as "unfair competition" a continuous practice of rifling news from a competitor and publishing it contemporaneously. To this we shall return;[64] the question here is the different and narrower one of copyright. Mr. Rovere's candid description of how other publishers rely on foreign dispatches of the New York *Times*[65] prepares us for the view which I have often heard stated by specialists (there is little case law), namely, that news, in the sense of the facts disclosed, is open to republication by anyone as long as the literary embellishments are not lifted.[66] According to this, the later newspaper publisher needs at most to interpose a rewrite man: compare the heavier burden falling on a later directory publisher. We can indeed expect the public interest attaching to rapid and easy circulation of news reports to engender a tolerant attitude toward copying them. A judge today would not put the result on a distinction between "originality" and "opportunity" as Judge Grosscup did in 1902;[67] one would expect him to say (even less informatively) that facts are in the public domain.[68] Yet it is possible for a court, incensed at some taking of news which it thinks particularly cheeky, to hold that "expression" has been lifted.

[63]International News Service v. Associated Press, 248 U.S. 215 (1918).

[64]See *infra*, Lecture III, pp. 86-87.

[65]See the quotation from Rovere in Lichtheim, *"All the News That's Fit to Print": Reflections on the New York Times*, 40 COMMENTARY, No. 3, at 33 (September 1965).

[66]See International News Service v. Associated Press, *supra* note 63, at 234; Gorman, *supra* note 60, at 1579; NIMMER, COPYRIGHT § 29.2 (1965).

[67]National Tel. News Co. v. Western Union Tel. Co., 119 Fed. 294 (7th Cir. 1902), mentioned *supra* p. 34.

[68]*Cf.* Davies v. Bowes, 209 Fed. 53 (S.D.N.Y. 1913), where a fictional "news story" lost all claim to copyright protection when set forth in the newspaper as a factual account (a "real life drama"). (The Davies case was affirmed on other grounds at 219 Fed. 178 [2d Cir. 1914].)

Also, if the significance of the news is minimal, a court may be tempted to treat it like data gathered for a directory and require a rival publisher to do his own work. This may be the unspoken key to Judge Wyzanski's decision in the *Triangle Publications* case[69] where he granted extremely broad continuing relief, under the title of copyright, against copying horseracing results, but yet purported to abide by Massachusetts law in refusing to follow the *I.N.S.* case.

It would be a difficult exercise to describe exactly what should figure as news and as the factual element in it. I can imagine news photographs that should be available for copying as "facts." Some public utterances should themselves qualify as facts so that newspapers should be allowed to publish them in full text, regardless of the authors' wishing otherwise or taking out formal copyrights. This liberty need not extend to publishing in permanent form,[70] though I can imagine situations in which that too should be free of restraint.

The factual content of histories is comparable to the nub of news, but the "expression" may be of great interest. Judge Hand laid it down in an early unpublished opinion that one might take and reproduce from a copyrighted history the facts recorded, even if the historian had come by them through his own hard digging. Nor could the historian, by recounting the facts chronologically, cut off the second-comer from this natural style of presentation. Judge Hand, indeed, went further and said: "There cannot be any such thing as copyright in the order of presentation of the facts, nor, indeed, in

[69] Triangle Pub., Inc. v. New England Newspaper Pub. Co., 46 F. Supp. 198 (D.Mass. 1942).

[70] See the suggestive dissenting opinion of Washington, C.J., in Public Affairs Associates, Inc. v. Rickover, 284 F.2d 262, 272 (D.C.Cir. 1960), *vacated for insufficient record,* 369 U.S. 111 (1962).

their selection, although into that selection may go the highest genius of authorship. . . ."[71] This formulation must have been out of abundant care to preserve access to the facts; it would leave only word-tracking or perhaps a too copious condensation or abridgment as actionable. A few recent cases seem a good deal less tolerant of the later writer, and especially, perhaps, if he attempts to popularize and thereby to cash in on recondite or laborious researches embodied in the predecessor work.[72] On any view it is preposterous to put any kind of fence around such facts, or any facts, for as long as fifty-six years, and no one can believe that a court would do so. But to avow that there is more liberty to copy as the original gets older may seem embarrassingly inconsistent with a statute that treats all copyrights with majestic equality as to duration.

Copying a copyrighted map embodying an important outcome of new field exploration would pose a nice question indeed, but the cases are not concerned with such productions. Some critics are despondent about recent intimations that no copyright can be held in a simple map consisting merely of a

[71]Myers v. The Mail & Express Co., No. E-15-138, S.D.N.Y., 23 July 1919, quoted in Brief for Appellant, pp. 36-37, Becker v. Loew's Inc., 133 F.2d 889 (7th Cir. 1943).

Through the courtesy of Samuel D. Cohen, Esq., of the New York Bar, I have been enabled to see the entire opinion in the Myers case and to place a copy on file in the Harvard Law Library.

[72]See Toksvig v. Bruce Pub. Co., 181 F.2d 664 (7th Cir. 1950); Holdredge v. Knight Pub. Corp., 214 F. Supp. 921 (S.D.Cal. 1963); cf. Eisenschiml v. Fawcett Pub., Inc., 246 F.2d 598 (7th Cir.), cert. denied, 355 U.S. 907 (1957).

I note with satisfaction that since the text was written the Second Circuit Court of Appeals, in litigation over a book about Howard Hughes, has questioned the correctness of the Toksvig decision and shown a more balanced attitude toward plagiarism in the field of history and biography. Rosemont Enterprises, Inc. v. Random House, Inc., 2d Cir., 17 August 1966, rev'g 150 U.S.P.Q. 367 (S.D.N.Y. 1966).

consolidation of older maps and supplying, perhaps, some minor information obtained by local inquiry or through books of reference.[73] These critics would prefer to allow the copyright but restrict its coverage to just the plaintiff's contribution.[74] But my earlier discussion suggested that a rule *de minimis* is natural and sound. Courts, moreover, may lose enthusiasm for giving any protection when they observe that the copyright notice in such cases is customarily blanket and does not inform the public how thin at best the copyright is or when they consider that there is a chance of excessive recovery[75] if the supposedly thin copyright is sustained and infringement found.

I jump to another part of the terrain. Quite naturally the copyright of a dramatic work now extends to its public performance, but *Baker v. Selden*,[76] the case of the bookkeeping systems, showed that the copyright of a work describing a practical art did not extend to the "performance" or exercise of the art, which remained free to all. Business schemes or methods are within the *Baker* rule. Sometimes a business scheme has tried (vainly) to masquerade as a dramatic composition—consider a plan for a roller-skating derby[77]—but what is an art or system within the reach of the *Baker* case is usually tolerably clear. In denying protection of the bookkeeping

[73]See Amsterdam v. Triangle Pub., Inc., 189 F.2d 104 (3d Cir. 1951); *but cf.* C.S. Hammond & Co. v. International College Globe, Inc., 210 F. Supp. 206 (S.D.N.Y. 1962). See Whicher, *Originality, Cartography, and Copyright*, 38 N.Y.U.L. REV. 280 (1963), reprinted in WHICHER, THE CREATIVE ARTS AND THE JUDICIAL PROCESS 33 (1965).
[74]See Gorman, *supra* note 60, at 1575-76.
[75]Notwithstanding the cases on "apportionment," see *infra* pp. 70-71.
[76]101 U.S. 99 (1879), *supra* p. 33.
[77]Seltzer v. Sunbrock, 22 F. Supp. 621 (S.D.Cal. 1938).

system, as such, I doubt that the *Baker* case was responding to a constitutional imperative, at least if the plaintiff was the actual originator of the system; and there are some who think business methods, if "elaborated" or "delineated,"[78] can, constitutionally, and should be made subjects of copyright in the sense of conferring the exclusive right of exercise. It is pointed out that the man who originated a workable system for producing and marketing paperbacks was more deserving than the authors or publishers of many sorry books put out in paperback which rest comfortably in copyright. Considering, however, the difficulties in demarking the limits of such copyrights of methods, and the pervasive intrusion on competition which would be threatened, I daresay most of us would prefer to stay with the *Baker* case.

Recall that the defendant was held free in the *Baker* case to sell forms similar to the plaintiff's. I think the privilege extends to exact copies,[79] for to require the person selling forms to bookkeepers to make changes in them to avoid technical infringement would seem a regrettable backsliding from the determination that the system was free for public use. The Supreme Court's late reference to the *Baker* case hardly helps on this question.[80] In the *Continental Casualty* case[81] recently decided by the Second Circuit, one Beardsley had copyrighted

[78]See Rubinstein, *Unfair Use of Elaborated Ideas*, 10 BULL. COPYR. SOC. 351 (1963).

[79]The Baker case indeed says in terms: "blank account-books are not the subject of copyright." 101 U.S. at 107.

[80]The reference is in Mazer v. Stein, 347 U.S. 201, 217 (1954), where the Court appears somewhat to misread the facts of the Baker case, but does make something of defendant Baker's having used "a different arrangement of the columns and . . . different headings."

[81]Continental Casualty Co. v. Beardsley, 253 F.2d 702 (2d Cir.), *cert. denied*, 358 U.S. 816 (1958).

an insurance plan including forms of bonds, affidavits, and other such gear. He charged the insurance company with using infringing forms to carry out the same plan. The court held Beardsley's forms copyrightable but said the standard of infringement would be so set as to bar only close imitation of the language, thereby allowing exploitation of the "ideas" back of the insurance plan. The forms had a good deal of lawyer's text, in this respect differing from the forms in the *Baker* case. Still the effect of the decision may be to force users to awkward and possibly dangerous recasting of the legal language to avoid infringement actions. In the court below, the judge would have gone the whole way and denied copyright to the forms.[82] I connect all this with the cases which refuse to allow copyright to be used to substitute for or enlarge the scope of a mechanical or process patent;[83] and I shall have to recall the present discussion in dealing in the third lecture with the question of copyrighting computer programs.

The question of architect's blueprints or drawings comes up as related to the *Baker* case with its distinction between "explanation" and "use." The statute lists as copyrightable works "models or designs for works of art" and the proprietor is given the exclusive right "to complete, execute, and finish" them.[84] Buildings, however, would be held not works of art, although monuments or separate decorations might be. This has both an illogic and a practical justification reminiscent of those encountered in discussing the configurations of dresses as subjects

[82]151 F. Supp. 28 (S.D.N.Y. 1957).
[83]See Brown Instrument Co. v. Warner, 161 F.2d 910 (D.C. Cir. 1947); Taylor Instrument Cos. v. Fawley-Brost Co., 139 F.2d 98 (7th Cir. 1943), *cert. denied,* 321 U.S. 785 (1944); Korzybski v. Underwood & Underwood, Inc., 36 F.2d 727 (2d Cir. 1929).
[84]17 U.S.C. §§ 5(g), 1(b) (1964).

of copyright.[85] With respect to buildings, then, we are remitted to the statutory provision for "drawings or plastic works of a scientific or technical character,"[86] but no right is given here to complete, execute or finish. So it appears that architect's drawings are to be somehow protected, but no protection is intended for the buildings, which may themselves be copied down to the last square foot of glass-front.[87] What, then, should copyright of the drawings be held to prevent? Unconsented-to reproduction as "explanation" in a book on architecture, yes; but not, I would suggest, reproduction for use in constructing a building.[88] On this view, which would put a limiting gloss, but a quite defensible one, on the general statutory prohibition against "copying," the copyright of the drawings would certainly be narrow. Let me add that I am not urging inferentially the creation of a full architectural copyright. Passing the question of what it would cover—the placement or ingredients of the electrical wiring or the plumbing fixtures?—I would point out that architecture is ordinarily a stable art in which a crowding of copyrights, damping down the customary copying among architects, might turn out embarrassing and stultifying.

To round out the examination of plagiarism, I shall comment on two general lines of authority thought to work against undue extension of that concept or rather of that congeries of concepts.

[85]*Supra* p. 55.
[86]17 U.S.C. § 5(i) (1964).
[87]See De Silva Construction Corp. v. Herrald, 213 F. Supp. 184, 195-96 (M.D.Fla. 1962); *cf.* Edgar H. Wood Assoc. v. Skene, 347 Mass. 351, 365, 197 N.E.2d 886, 895 (1964).
[88]*Compare* Muller v. Triborough Bridge Authority, 43 F. Supp. 298, 299 (S.D.N.Y. 1942), *with* May v. Bray, 30 C.O. Bull. 435, 436 (S.D.Cal. 1955), and Edgar H. Wood Assoc. v. Skene, *supra* note 87. See *infra*, Lecture III, p. 85, n. 19, on the problem of "publication" of plans.

First, "fair use." Does this doctrine—a floating one, not mentioned in the statute—bring into our inquiry anything new or special? We are told that the earliest American report in which the expression fair use appeared—within quotation marks—was that of *Lawrence v. Dana*[89] in 1869, where the defendant's edition of Wharton's *Elements of International Law* was accused as a plagiarism of the plaintiff's earlier edition of the same work. Justice Clifford's opinion, sustaining the charge, followed Story on the factors to be considered in adjudging liability for the research uses of one scholarly book by another;[90] fair use emerged as the sort of taking which on such consideration would be held noninfringing. Justice Clifford was not being consciously innovative. Judge Hand in the *Nichols* and *Sheldon* cases seemed also to speak of fair use as merely the contrary of infringement.[91] But other authorities have taken fair use to refer to a set of justifications averting liability for what on the face of things is infringement.[92] This tends to leave the impression that infringement itself is decided without contamination by notions of policy, with fair use coming in later to supply those notions. But policy runs throughout our subject, as much of the discourse to this point shows. Dealing with fact works, Professor Gorman does not apply fair use as a separate analytical instrument;[93] it would,

[89]15 Fed. Cas. 26, 60 (No. 8136) (C.C.D.Mass. 1869). On early usages of fair use or cognate expressions, see Cohen, *Fair Use in the Law of Copyright*, in 6 ASCAP, COPYRIGHT LAW SYMPOSIUM 43, 48-49 (1955).

[90]Justice Clifford relied particularly on Folsom v. Marsh, 9 Fed. Cas. 342, 348 (No. 4901) (C.C.D.Mass. 1841).

[91]Nichols v. Universal Pictures Corp., 45 F.2d 119, 121 (2d Cir. 1930), *cert. denied,* 282 U.S. 902 (1931); Sheldon v. Metro-Goldwyn Pictures Corp., 81 F.2d 49, 54 (2d Cir.), *cert. denied,* 298 U.S. 669 (1936).

[92]NIMMER, COPYRIGHT § 145, at 645 (1965). See generally Cohen, *supra* note 89, at 45-48.

[93]See Gorman, *Copyright Protection for the Collection and Representation of Facts,* 76 HARV. L. REV. 1569, 1602-05 & n. 136 (1963).

I think, be possible to dispense with it in relation to other works also.

We will indeed find little in the interesting review of fair use by Mr. Latman[94] for which our previous thinking has not prepared us. There is particular stress on the purpose of the taking as conditioning liability. Thus copying a work for one's own use—for example, transcribing passages of a treatise for study purpose—has generally been thought, unsurprisingly enough, to raise no question;[95] anyway it was a question no one would be interested to litigate. Then photocopying loomed. This phenomenon we shall finally have to consider.[96] Cases of "incidental use"—say the quotation in stories or essays of old copyrighted song-lyrics as means of recalling the spirit of the times[97]—remind us of the point already made that copyrighted works are in one aspect themselves "facts" or events of history. On the edge of "incidental use" we find cases where the sting is perhaps not copyright infringement at all; a few sentences from a scientific paper, together with the author's name, are quoted in a pamphlet about cigarettes: what the author may be really complaining about, though he successfully invokes his copyright, is the implication that he consented to quotation for a fee.[98] Incidental use is close to a strange or unexpected one, and I therefore put the case of the Scottish poet Hugh MacDiarmid who took part of a para-

[94]Latman, *Fair Use of Copyrighted Works,* Study No. 14 Prepared for the Subcommittee on Patents, Trademarks, and Copyrights of the Senate Comm. on the Judiciary, 86th Cong., 2d Sess. (Comm. Print 1960).

[95]*But cf.* WEIL, AMERICAN COPYRIGHT LAW 406 (1917).

[96]See *infra,* Lecture III, pp. 101-2.

[97]Broadway Music Corp. v. F-R Pub. Corp., 31 F. Supp. 817 (S.D.N.Y. 1940).

[98]Henry Holt & Co., Inc. v. Liggett & Myers Tobacco Co., 23 F. Supp. 302 (E.D.Pa. 1938).

graph in a copyrighted novel by Glyn Jones, broke it up into lines, and published it as a poem under the title "Perfect."[99] I do not like MacDiarmid's failure to acknowledge the source, if he was in fact conscious of taking from Jones; otherwise I would not despair of writing a brief for MacDiarmid. Again, the right to do a parody of a work without permission of the copyright proprietor seems as clear in reason as the right to reproduce excerpts from a copyrighted work for purposes of criticism or, for that matter, to refer to such a work in an index or catalogue. I will not conceal my view that it was wrong— and possibly unconstitutional—to hold Jack Benny for his television parody of the movie *Gaslight*.[100] The courts presumably went on the ground that Benny had taken more material direct from the movie than parody really required.[101] But parody generally requires a reprise of the original; this may have to be extensive when the audience is not very knowledgeable. Moreover we must accept the harsh truth that parody may quite legitimately aim at garroting the original, destroying it commercially as well as artistically. The Second Circuit has recently spoken some good sense in this vein about parody while exonerating *Mad Magazine* for a spoof of popular songs.[102] But without multiplying examples I recur to the point

[99]This is but one version of the facts. The hullabaloo over MacDiarmid is best followed in 1964 TIMES LITERARY SUPP. 1178; 1965 *id.* 47, 67, 87, 107, 127, 147, 215, 311, 331, 351, 371, 391. See also Lewis, *Prose into Poetry*, N.Y. Times Book Rev., 12 September 1965, at 2.

[100]Benny v. Loew's Inc., 239 F.2d 532 (9th Cir. 1956), *aff'd by an equally divided court, without opinion, sub nom.* Columbia Broadcasting System, Inc. v. Loew's Inc., 356 U.S. 43 (1958).

[101]See Carter, D.J., in Columbia Pictures Corp. v. National Broadcasting Co., 137 F. Supp. 348, 351 (S.D.Cal. 1955).

[102]Berlin v. E. C. Publications, Inc., 329 F.2d 541 (2d Cir.), *cert. denied,* 379 U.S. 822 (1964).

that "fair use" invokes policy as does the rest of the subject of plagiarism and in no markedly different sense.

Second, I shall touch on modulations of the remedies for copyright infringement. In *Haas v. Leo Feist, Inc.*,[103] one of the defendant's employees had taken the plaintiff's song "You Will Never Know How Much I Really Cared" and made it over into the rousing success "I Didn't Raise My Boy to Be a Soldier." The copying was in the music of the chorus; the words of the two songs did not match at all. Judge Hand said it was "perfectly apparent to unsophisticated common-sense that the song's success was due to its sentiment and its appositeness to a certain strain of popular feeling at the time." Yet he thought himself bound by precedent to award the net profits earned by the defendant from the whole of the infring-ing song—not merely so much of those profits as was traceable to the copied music.[104] (There were in fact no "damages" to the plaintiff, as distinguished from "profits" of the defendant.) Now on principle it seems that recovery should be only of the part of the defendant's gains attributable to the material wrong-fully lifted from the plaintiff's work. In the *Sheldon* case on second appeal to the Circuit Court of Appeals,[105] two decades after the *Haas* case, the question of making this kind of ap-portionment arose in poignant form. For, as we know, the defendants' picture contained only a fraction of the fraction of plaintiff's play which could be called original, and that not in the same words; and according to the rough-and-tumble speculations that masquerade as the science of legal cause-

---

[103]234 Fed. 105 (S.D.N.Y. 1916).

[104]Here and below, in discussing the Haas case, I omit mention of estoppel as bearing on the recovery. In the end the plaintiff failed because of a defect in the notice of copyright inscribed on the music.

[105]106 F.2d 45 (1939).

and-effect, it seemed that by far the larger part of the defend-ants' profits must have resulted not from the infringing mate-rial in the picture but from the popularity of the advertised star performers (Joan Crawford and Robert Montgomery), from the production and direction, and other things. Judge Hand, overruling the old authority, now held that the plaintiffs were entitled to but 20 percent of the defendants' net profits. The Supreme Court affirmed with an opinion by Chief Justice Hughes.[106] Apportionment, however, is not available auto-matically whenever the defendant's work is only partly an infringement; the defendant must somehow contrive to show how the offending part can be disentangled from the rest and in what degree it contributed to the profits. "Strictly and liter-ally it is true that the problem is insoluble."[107] In practice niceties must be overlooked and considerable imprecision ac-cepted in fixing the magic percentage which is at once to save the defendant from gross overcharge and—at least where the infringement is viewed as "deliberate"—to "favor the . . . [plaintiff] in every reasonable chance of error."[108] Now the second incarnation of the *Sheldon* case, the accounting phase, does not reconcile me to the first, the initial holding of infringe-ment. It has been suggested that a rule of apportionment, by softening the remedy, encourages people to infringe, but I venture the thought that it may seduce judges into finding infringement in dubious cases by holding out some assurance that the defendant will anyway not be hit too hard.

[106]309 U.S. 390 (1940).

[107]Sheldon v. Metro-Goldwyn Pictures Corp., 106 F.2d at 48.

[108]*Id.* at 51. See Orgel v. Clark Boardman Co., Ltd., 301 F.2d 119 (2d Cir.), *cert. denied*, 371 U.S. 817 (1962), *modifying* 128 U.S.P.Q. 531 (S.D.N.Y. 1960). *But cf.* Alfred Bell & Co., Ltd. v. Catalda Fine Arts, Inc., 86 F. Supp. 399, 410 (S.D.N.Y. 1949), *aff'd*, 191 F.2d 99 (2d Cir. 1951).

The *Haas* case posed the question whether the *quo animo* of the defendant should influence monetary recoveries. Presumably the defendant music publisher had not known or had ground to suspect the composer's plagiarism. Judge Hand said innocence would not relieve of damages; curiously, he was rather less clear about the bearing of innocence on a recovery of profits, but concluded that it would not in itself relieve. The irrelevance of innocence he thought a consequence of the statutory notice which charged everyone with knowledge; otherwise, imposing liability without blameworthiness could not, he thought, be justified on general tort principles. But on a realistic view, how did the presence of a notice on the plaintiff's obscure song make any difference to the unknowing defendant? In *Barry v. Hughes,*[109] Judge Hand observed *obiter* that innocence might excuse damages, but probably not liability for what he called "unjust enrichment." The problem arose for decision in *De Acosta v. Brown,*[110] and here Judge Hand was reduced to dissent. The whole court agreed that there was no escape from the accounting for profits (and I agree, on reasoning as old as Aristotle, that profits are harder to excuse than damages[111]). As to damages, Hand was alone in thinking they should not be exacted from an innocent defendant. But he stressed that he was talking about the kind of innocence that happened to be involved in both the *Barry* and *De Acosta* cases (possibly it was involved also in *Haas*): the defendant published with a stranger's license what appeared to be the stranger's work but was in fact a copy of the plaintiff's

[109]103 F.2d 427 (2d Cir.), *cert. denied,* 308 U.S. 604 (1939).
[110]146 F.2d 408 (2d Cir. 1944), *cert. denied,* 325 U.S. 862 (1945).
[111]See FULLER & BRAUCHER, BASIC CONTRACT LAW 42 (1964), for discussion of the fifth chapter of the Nicomachean Ethics.

work. Hand thought the damage liability in such circumstances would be "unique in severity" and might prove "an appreciable incubus upon the freedom of the press." But I fail to see how Hand provided a satisfying basis for distinguishing other cases of innocence, right back to the case of Jerome Kern's unconscious lifting from "Dardanella." I doubt that a distinction appears if we ask what preventive measures the defendants might have taken if aware of a severe rule of liability.[112] Rules on conversion of ordinary personalty came in for considerable discussion in the *De Acosta case.* I agree that copyright questions should not live behind palisades of parochialism; they should be constantly measured against general principle; but there is at the same time a danger of assimilating too easily the case of a man unknowingly taking a gold watch with that of a bookseller selling a book which, unknown to him, contains a plagiarism.

To speak at large about the copyright remedies, while their nature and interrelationships are coming to be better understood, there is still a lack of flexibility in molding them to the offense and occasion. For example, courts have sometimes forgotten that an injuction does not go of course; the interest in dissemination of a work may justify a confinement of the remedy to a money recovery (just as it may suggest the legislative use, in proper doses, of the device of a compulsory license).[113] To the rigidities the courts bring upon themselves, must be added those forced on them by the difficult and, in

[112]Compare the careful opinion in Shapiro, Bernstein & Co., Inc. v. H. L. Green Co., Inc., 316 F.2d 304 (2d Cir. 1963).

[113]A late instance of the unfortunate grant of a preliminary injunction was the action of the District Court in the Howard Hughes litigation, soundly reversed by the Court of Appeals. See *supra* note 72.

places, nearly impenetrable provisions for "in lieu" damages, that is, fixed damages.[114]

Examining the view from the top of the hill, I find one temptation easy to resist, and that is to sum up copyright with just the word "property" or "personality" or any one of the other essences to which scholars, foreign and domestic, have been trying to reduce the subject since before the time of Mansfield. To say that copyright is "property," although a fundamentally unhistorical statement, would not be baldly misdescriptive if one were prepared to acknowledge that there is property *and* property, with few if any legal consequences extending uniformly to all species and that in practice the lively questions are likely to be whether certain consequences ought to attach to a given piece of so-called property in given circumstances. In the same way we might make do with "personality" or some other general characterization of copyright. But characterization in grand terms then seems of little value: we may as well go directly to the policies actuating or justifying the particular determinations.

Copyright law wants to give any necessary support and encouragement to the creation and dissemination of fresh signals or messages to stir human intelligence and sensibilities: it recognizes the importance of these excitations for the development of individuals and society. Especially is copyright directed to those kinds of signals which are in their nature "fragile"—so easy of replication that incentive to produce would be quashed by the prospect of rampant reproduction by freeloaders. To these signals copyright affords what I have

[114]17 U.S.C. § 101(b); see the heroic interpretive opinion of Judge Feinberg in Davis v. E. I. du Pont de Nemours & Co., 249 F. Supp. 471 (S.D. N.Y. 1966).

called "headstart," that is, a group of rights amounting to a qualified monopoly running for a limited time. The legal device has been considered not too complex for administrative purposes and on the whole easier to handle than alternatives such as government subventions.

I have spoken of encouraging "creation" as well as "dissemination," but copyright has evidently more to do today with mobilizing the profit-propelled apparatus of dissemination—publication and distribution—than with calling the signals into first unpublished existence; the latter process must be to a considerable extent self-generated. But copyright tends also to serve the material expectations and psychological cravings of the individual creative worker: it gives him an opportunity (though by no means the certainty) of reward for his efforts; conventional recognition for the feat of creating a work; a means (though not a very good one) of preserving the artistic integrity of the work through controlling its exploitation.

The headstart conferred (which is the encouragement given, the inducement held out) should be moderate in all its dimensions. Magnify the headstart and you may conceivably run the risk of attracting too much of the nation's energy into the copyright-protected sectors of the economy. But more serious is the danger of hobbling unduly the reception and enjoyment of the signals by their potential audience, or of clogging the utilization of the signals by other authors in the creation of further or improved signals for additional audiences.[115] Eliciting publication is not an end in itself. Publication without easy access to the product would defeat the social

---

[115]Copyright protection could thus ultimately meet the same constitutional objections as other attempted restraints on expression. See *supra* note 100 and accompanying text.

purpose of copyright already mentioned as primary. Beyond this, various additional social needs and demands strive to make themselves felt to modulate and qualify the headstart as we move from one to another of the types of works covered by copyright.

We are back to the public aspect of the headstart and of this whole branch of law—to be remembered even in the most commonplace action to enforce copyright. Our gaze should not be confined to *this* plaintiff and *this* defendant. If the contest is conceived as being thus restricted, a court out of understandable sympathy would be inclined to hold for the plaintiff whenever the defendant was shown to have made any recognizable use of the plaintiff's contribution. That would be a very mistaken attitude. There is a further diffused public interest necessarily involved.

As the rules of the game about plagiarism determine, indeed are, part of the outline of the headstart, they should respond at every point to the interacting policies. They do not. They tend to look in upon themselves and forget their public obligations. The phenomenon is omnipresent: no body of law can remain in constant, sensitive accord with its essential justifications; the very array of rules, subrules, parables, proverbs, metaphors, and procedures invented to make the law readily usable, must to some extent compel it to belie its genius. So with plagiarism: the intensity of the search to find what was the plaintiff's original contribution, then to judge whether that was somehow taken by the defendant—the unavoidable matching of negative entropies—has sometimes driven out other considerations. When thus detached, the law of plagiarism drifts toward excessive protection, with reciprocal excessive constraint, out of proportion to any needed incentive to the producer (the major consideration), and unjustified by any collateral objectives of copyright.

I am far from suggesting that the law is undergoing a general, wicked deterioration. That wily gentleman, common-law process, has been carrying on with spirit in his usual patchy way. After some wavering, he has answered sensibly the question what is to be considered a fresh signal, which is to ask what is authorship for copyright purposes. So, too, he has apprehended pretty clearly, most of the time, that copyright should not withdraw from the common store building blocks necessary to composition—small particular sequences and general concepts. The great in-between is the playground of the quest for the "identity" and thus for the "sameness" of works; this must start with a judgment about where the interest in the work lies, and the variableness of the judgment is clear if you ask yourself what a Hottentot would see in *Hamlet*. I have dared to suggest that it is unfortunate to take Judge Hand's "patterning" metaphor as embodying a truth rather than merely an interesting style of analysis, or, viewing it even in the latter sense, to give it too wide a range of application. Ignoring functional differences between works, distinctions between imaginative works and others, or among the types making up these big divisions, remains a vice, although not as common as in times past. It is a question of sinning against flexibility by unwillingness to look closely at the works or to admit considerations of policy beyond the immediately obvious. We find irresolution about when copyright interests are to yield and let go as they enter stronger fields of force: I remind you of insurance forms and architect's plans. Copyright still suffers from excessive reification, the assumption that because a copyright behaves like ordinary personal property for one or more purposes, it must so behave for all. I have barely hinted that copyright proves but an awkward defender of artistic integrity: perhaps the dependence on copyright for the purpose has inhibited the growth of decent protective law under other auspices.[116]

I conclude with the observation that when copyright has gone wrong in recent times, it has been by taking itself too seriously, by foolish assumptions about the amount of originality open to man as an artificer, by sanctimonious pretensions about the iniquities of imitation. I confess myself to be more worried about excessive than insufficient protection, and follow Voltaire in thinking that plagiarism, even at its worst, *"est assurément de tous les larcins le moins dangereux pour la société."*[117]

[116]Strauss, *The Moral Right of the Author*, Study No. 4 Prepared for the Subcommittee on Patents, Trademarks, and Copyrights of the Senate Comm. on the Judiciary, 86th Cong., 2d Sess. (Comm. Print 1960).

[117]DICTIONNAIRE PHILOSOPHIQUE under title "Plagiat," in 42 OEUVRES COMPLÈTES DE VOLTAIRE 321 (Imprimerie de la Société Littéraire-Typographique 1784).

III. Proposals and Prospects

WE COME at length to proposals to reform the Copyright Act, which is in large part still the statute as approved on 4 March 1909. It is time to redo this Edwardian enactment, and, besides improving generally the rheumatic text, we need, *first*, to rationalize the formal requirements of the law which in one way or another condition access to substantive benefits (I refer here to the formalities of notice, registration, deposit, recordation of transfers); *second*, to deal with various forms of protection cognate to copyright that have grown up in an unprincipled way outside the federal statute; *third*, to meet acute issues between producers and users arising largely from the revolutionary new methods of transmitting and replicating signals. In discussing these and related matters I shall, when possible, use as a base, as a *point d'appui*, the Revision Bill now pending in Congress[1]—a conscientious, highly expert

[1] The reference is to the revision bill of 1965, H.R. 4347, 89th Cong., 1st Sess. [hereinafter cited as Revision Bill]. This Bill, together with the 1964 revision bill, a 1963 "preliminary draft," and the text of the current law, is reproduced in REGISTER OF COPYRIGHTS, COPYRIGHT LAW REVISION, PT. 6, SUPPLEMENTARY REPORT ON THE GENERAL REVISION OF THE U.S. COPYRIGHT LAW: 1965 REVISION BILL, printed for the use of the House Committee on the Judiciary, 89th Cong., 1st Sess. (Comm. Print 1965) [hereinafter cited as COPYRIGHT LAW REVISION, PT. 6].

The Revision Bill was introduced by Congressman Celler on 4 February

draft sponsored by the Register of Copyrights as head of the
Copyright Office. I shall close the lectures by invoking the
longer-range future of copyright.

First, the formalities. There is no escaping this dusty
subject. It is far from trivial for us; traditionally it has nearly
transfixed us; and I must report that the formalities still engage
about one-third of the text of the Revision Bill.

Debate on formalities has a way of getting caught up in
the high-flown quarrel whether copyright is a "natural" or an
"artificial" right. When we descend from the empyrean, we
see that our elaborate formalities simply help to some degree
in making transactions with copyrights more secure. But it is
inherently difficult to keep track of these airy properties: the
process is cumbersome and the results very imperfect. In the
effort to force people to toe the mark of the formalities, there
has been a regrettable tendency to exact forfeitures for venial
omissions; I remind you of the early great case of *Wheaton v.
Peters*.[2] Although I am well convinced that the country would
survive a scuttling of all the formalities, I see fair cause for
retaining them if the new act follows the precept of assessing

---

1965. Hearings on the Bill were held intermittently in May, June, August,
and September 1965 and are reported in *Hearings Before Subcommittee
No. 3 of the House Committee on the Judiciary*, 89th Cong., 1st Sess., ser.
8, Pts. 1-3 (1966) [hereinafter cited as *House Hearings*]. Hearings by a
Subcommittee on Patents, Trademarks, and Copyrights of the Senate
Judiciary Committee on a parallel bill, S. 1006, were begun in August 1965
but soon suspended.

As of the date of sending this manuscript to press, the House subcommittee has held numerous executive sessions with a view to making recom-
mendations to the full committee. On 5 May 1966 it issued a statement of
its intentions on the subject of CATV. In August 1966 the Senate subcommittee resumed hearings to consider the same subject. See *infra* note 79.

[2] 33 U.S. (8 Pet.) 591 (1834), discussed *supra* pp. 26-27.

what they are truly worth and properly modulating the penalties (which can of course be restated as rewards).

I shall leave to my footnotes the formalities of deposit of specimen copies[3] and recordation of transfers of copyright interests,[4] and speak of my precept first in regard to the notice supposed to be inscribed on published works. (Everyone recalls seeing the line "Copyright © 1966 by John Smith" on the verso of the title pages of books.) The notice is now a complicated but nevertheless a do-or-die requirement, and I could a sad tale unfold of cruel forfeitures. Judges, however, who in recent times have inclined against brutality, have run the risk of appearing slightly ridiculous in their tortuous interpretations. Thus Judge Hand held in the *Peter Pan* case[5] that a notice for a fabric design was adequate despite the fact that it was stamped on the selvage of the cloth and would disappear when the cloth was made up into the dresses for which it was destined. The values claimed for the notice—that when present, it imparts useful, cautionary information, and when absent, releases to the public domain material no one is

[3]The deposit formality helps the Library of Congress collections. Under the Revision Bill, §406, failure to deposit would be subject to sanction, but would not alone destroy a copyright, as today it can. 17 U.S.C. §§13, 14 (1964).

[4]The Revision Bill properly views recordation together with initial registration as intended to provide continuous running information. It is the threatening figure of the bona fide purchaser who wields the sanctions regarding recordation, and they are stiff. Acknowledging the difficulties of preserving a connected history of transactions with a copyright, the Revision Bill not only tries to insist on better identification of affected works but makes the constructive notice arising from recordation turn to some extent upon what a putative reasonable search of the public records would have revealed. Revision Bill §205 (c)(1).

[5]Peter Pan Fabrics, Inc. v. Martin Weiner Corp., 274 F.2d 487 (2d Cir. 1960). See also H.M. Kolbe Co., Inc. v. Armgus Textile Co., Inc., 315 F.2d 70 (2d Cir. 1963).

interested to own—these values are subject to discount in many situations. For a notice may be valid, though it misleads;[6] and copyright may be in force, though the work has circulated without notice.[7] The Revision Bill does not, and I think cannot, measurably heighten the achievement of the claimed values, but it does simplify the notice proper,[8] and in case of breach of the notice requirement it tries to deprive the owner of remedies for uses of the work by other persons only to the extent of the justifiable reliance by those others on the misprision.[9] This is right, but hard to carry out with fidelity. Here I go along generally with the Bill, but I am repelled by a provision which would, in certain events of lack of notice combined with failure to register, totally invalidate the copyright.[10] It really carries forms too far to give them hanging importance.

Registration consists of the submission by the copyright claimant of basic facts and material; these the Copyright Office examines for evident signs of uncopyrightability or other defects; if the Office finds none, it issues a certificate which has prima facie effects in litigation. The process lays down a public record and brings works under official security; and though the record is supplied ex parte and the official look is very superficial, there is value in both. Registration is a condition of an action for infringement, but it has been held that it may be accomplished tardily, on the eve of suit.[11]

[6]A mild example is Wrench v. Universal Pictures Co., Inc., 104 F. Supp. 374 (S.D.N.Y. 1952).

[7]As where it was circulated without authority of the copyright proprietor. Cf. 17 U.S.C. §10 (1964).

[8]See Revision Bill §401, esp. subsection (c).

[9]Revision Bill §404 (b).

[10]Revision Bill §404(a).

[1] Washingtonian Publishing Co., Inc. v. Pearson, 306 U.S. 30 (1939).

Although proprietors could thus get away with late registration or even none at all, registrations continue to be made fairly promptly and in large numbers—in part, I suppose, because producers want to show potential users a shipshape record. In the Revision Bill there is a commendable but awkward attempt to adjust the prima facie effect of the certificate to the time of registration; more important, the Bill would increase the stimulus to early registration by adopting a general rule of cutting off awards of statute-fixed damages and attorney's fees for infringements occurring before registration.[12]

We shall see that the copyright contemplated by the Revision Bill would generally take hold from the time of creation of a work, not from its distribution in tangible copies, as is generally the case under the present act. Correspondingly, the Bill permits registration at any time after creation.[13] Notice, however, is still tied to "hard" copies.[14] Under the new technology, many exploited works will never, or only ultimately or marginally, be distributed in hard form. So registration may take on greater importance, and this tends to reconcile us to the stepped-up sanctions. But it is just at this point that we may begin to wonder whether the formalities in their detailed prescriptions can long remain relevant to the highly fluid communications systems now burgeoning. Probably not. Later I shall return to the question of how to make the law respond to rapidly changing conditions.

To pass to the second subject, what I have called an unprincipled extension of protection has come about, in part,

[12]Revision Bill §§409(c), 411.
[13]Revision Bill §407(a).
[14]Revision Bill §§401(a), 402(a).

through a twistification of "publication," a concept which has been crucial in copyright law since the Statute of Anne.

Of old our national copyright statute pitched upon works at the point of publication; it had little to say about them while in unpublished status. If an author kept his manuscript in his desk drawer or circulated it only among his close friends, he was indeed protected against another who laid hold of the work and copied or otherwise exploited it without permission. The protection, however, did not spring from the statute but from common law: it went by the title of "common-law copyright." This copyright was thought to continue as long as the work remained unpublished; it was thus without limit of time. When the author published, which betokened exploitation of the work on his part, he must, by following prescribed forms, submit himself to the statute, which then molded and limited his monopoly in the name of the public interest; if he did not so submit, he forfeited all rights.

Multiplication and general distribution of printed copies was surely a publication; but what of public performance or representation, say of a play? If exploitation is the key, this should rank as publication. In *Ferris v. Frohman*,[15] however, the Supreme Court through Justice Hughes held in 1912 that despite numerous commercial performances all over the country, an unprinted play, *The Fatal Card*, remained unpublished: the proprietors, who had made no attempt to go under the statute, still retained the common-law copyright and could bring their common-law action for infringement.

I shall not pause to explain the curious English genealogy

[15]223 U.S. 424 (1912).

of the *Ferris* rule.[16] (The rule well illustrates how our law concentrated itself upon the model case of the conventional book distributed in copies and ran into trouble dealing with variant situations.) A new provision of the act of 1909 for securing copyright of plays, music, and certain other works while yet unprinted,[17] did not dislodge the *Ferris* proposition; so we have today a state of affairs in which a playwright or composer not interested in multiplying copies can hold an 'indeterminate monopoly by simply snuggling up to the common law and ignoring the statute. It is not merely a matter of "perpetual" as against limited duration of rights; the copyright statute has a considerable number of other controls and limits which may be thus circumvented. Now I must add that the *Ferris* doctrine exerts or may claim to exert dominion precisely in the field of the media which are ringleaders in the communications revolution, media like radio or television which attain their effects without replicating hard copies.[18] It has been contended that even public sale of phonograph records or tapes does not publish the underlying works, and some question has been raised about the time, if any, when motion pictures, distributed by leasing in the usual way, figure as published.[19]

[16]See Selvin, *Should Performance Dedicate?*, 42 CALIF. L. REV. 40 (1954); Kaplan, *Publication in Copyright Law: The Question of Phonograph Records*, 103 U. PA. L. REV. 469, 474-75 (1955).

[17]Copyright Act of 1909, §11, now 17 U.S.C. §12 (1964).

[18]The question was lately renewed in King v. Mister Maestro, Inc., 224 F. Supp. 101 (S.D.N.Y. 1963).

[19]These matters are discussed by Kaplan, *supra* note 16; Nimmer, *Copyright Publication*, 56 COLUM. L. REV. 185, 188-94, 197-98 (1956).

Somewhat related is the question whether architect's plans are divestitively published by required filing in a local record office or by construction

So much for abuse of the concept of "publication" as a regrettable means of sidestepping the statute. Another, more complex end-run around the statute starts with the *I.N.S.* case.[20] When in November 1916 the International News Service for sundry misdemeanors was denied use of the cables from the war front, it commenced to take and flash to its members the substance of Associated Press dispatches culled from A.P. bulletin boards or A.P. member newspapers on the Eastern seaboard. This annoyed A.P. because it enabled some I.N.S. papers in the West to beat their A.P. rivals to the street with A.P. news not labeled as such. In suing to stop this continuing practice, A.P. did not rely on the Copyright Act, since it had not attempted copyright of the dispatches; and even if that had been tried, taking the gist of the news would probably have been held not an infringement. The Supreme Court (with Justices McKenna, Holmes, and Brandeis disagreeing) nevertheless chose to create a kind of "property" in A.P., and correspondingly to cut down free access to the information, by enjoining I.N.S. (I quote from the decree) from "gainfully using . . . [A.P.'s] news, either bodily or in substance . . . until its commercial value as news to . . . [A.P.] and all of its members has passed away." The majority opinion, presumably reacting to the argument "either copyright or nothing," tried to describe the wrong as something different

and exhibition of the building proper. Compare De Silva Construction Corp. v. Herrald, 213 F. Supp. 184 (M.D.Fla. 1962), with Edgar H. Wood Associates, Inc. v. Skene, 347 Mass. 351, 197 N.E.2d 886 (1964). As to possible divestitive publication of a painting by display in a public gallery, see American Tobacco Co. v. Werckmeister, 207 U.S. 284 (1907); Werckmeister v. American Lithographic Co., 134 Fed. 321 (2d Cir. 1904); Pierce & Bushnell Mfg. Co. v. Werckmeister, 72 Fed. 54 (1st Cir. 1896).
   [20]International News Service v. Associated Press, 248 U.S. 215 (1918).

from copying: it lay, according to the opinion, in the defendant's tapping the plaintiff's facilities for gathering and distributing news, rather than in merely lifting the news. Nor, said the Court, was a copyright-like monopoly being conferred outside the statute: protection was after all to run for a short time and only against a competitor. The title "unfair competition" was invoked, but in a new sense of misappropriation rather than misrepresentation or passing off.

In the retrospect of nearly fifty years, the peculiarly strong sympathetic appeal of the facts for A.P. comes through undimmed, but we see also the wisdom of Professor Kocourek's objection at the time[21] that the limits, which is to say the exact policy justifications, of the new doctrine were so hard to describe that the well-wishing adventurer might pause before setting forth. The case opened an uncertain vista of liability for "reaping the fruits of . . . [one's competitor's] efforts and expenditure,"[22] that is, for doing what one constantly does by various forms of imitation of noncopyrighted, nonpatented material.

There is a letter from Judge Hand to Justice Brandeis written shortly after the *I.N.S.* decision saying that he would have sided with the majority.[23] But his attitude changed to one of measured hostility to the *I.N.S.* doctrine, as shown in three cases through 1940 in which plaintiffs sought to stop "reaping" or "unfair competition" similar to that in *I.N.S.*, although perhaps not so destructive in effect. In the *Cheney* case,[24] the defendant was lifting the plaintiff's original designs

[21]Note, 13 ILL. L. REV. 708 (1919).
[22]248 U.S. at 241.
[23]The letter, dated 22 January 1919, is reproduced in part in MASON, BRANDEIS: A FREE MAN'S LIFE 579 n. (1946).
[24]Cheney Bros. v. Doris Silk Corp., 35 F.2d 279 (2d Cir. 1929), *cert. denied*, 281 U.S. 728 (1930).

printed on silk goods. In the *Fashion Originators* case,[25] the subject was dress designs. In the *Whiteman* case,[26] the defendant radio station bought phonograph records manufactured and distributed by the plaintiff R.C.A. which carried popular music as performed by Whiteman and his orchestra; an injunction was sought against the defendant's playing the plaintiff's works over the air—by the "plaintiff's works" I mean not the notational music belonging to the composers, but Whiteman's performances or renditions as captured on the records. In none of the cases had the plaintiff resorted to federal statute; copyright was not available for silk prints before *Mazer v. Stein* (decided in 1954),[27] and is still not available for dress designs or recorded performances. Judge Hand denied relief in all three cases. He considered *I.N.S.* as a case "where the occasion is at once the justification for, and the limit of, what is decided." (What a strange case such a case would be!) He said, "The difficulties of understanding it otherwise are insuperable."[28] To follow *I.N.S.* and construct a kind of irregular patent or copyright, whether it be called "unfair competition" or something else, "would flagrantly conflict with the scheme which Congress has for more than a century devised to cover the subject-matter."[29] This view was reinforced by a prevision of the difficulties that would arise in conditioning the anomalous rights—should it be done

[25]Fashion Originators Guild v. FTC, 114 F.2d 80 (2d Cir. 1940), *aff'd*, 312 U.S. 457 (1941) (discusses the bearing of the old English authorities).
[26]R.C.A. Mfg. Co., Inc. v. Whiteman, 114 F.2d 86 (2d Cir.), *cert. denied*, 311 U.S. 712 (1940).
[27]347 U.S. 201 (1954).
[28]Cheney Bros. v. Doris Silk Corp., 35 F.2d 279, 280 (2d Cir. 1929), *cert. denied*, 281 U.S. 728 (1930).
[29]*Ibid.*

in tune with statute or in some other way? Here Judge Hand thought Justice Brandeis's reasons, elaborated in his *I.N.S.* dissent, for remitting news piracy to Congress, were compelling also for the courts' keeping their hands off design and record piracy. The solecism contended for could not be made pardonable by simply keeping it small, as by limiting the injunction for a seasonal design to the season.

I want to stress that Judge Hand in this triad of cases was looking at the monopoly statute, the Copyright Act, as a "scheme" which must be taken as complete. "An omission [from the statute] in such cases," he said, "must be taken to have been as deliberate as though it were express, certainly after long-standing action on the subject-matter."[30] But if a negative arose by implication from the federal enactment itself, no room at all would be left for a state rule, judicial or statutory, purporting—if we take the *Whiteman* case as an example—to protect recorded performances against public broadcast: the statute would control as "supreme law," and the doctrine of *Erie R.R. v. Tompkins*,[31] decided in 1938, two years before *Whiteman*, would be irrelevant.

This point of implication from the statute seems overlooked in the *Capitol Records* case which came to the Second Circuit in 1955.[32] In structure the case was like *Whiteman* except for the fact, highly sympathetic for the plaintiff, that the defendant was not attempting merely to play the records publicly but rather to duplicate records from a matrix record. A majority of the court, finding that Congress, although em-

[30]*Id.* at 281.
[31]304 U.S. 64 (1938).
[32]Capitol Records, Inc. v. Mercury Records Corp., 221 F.2d 657 (2d Cir. 1955).

powered to legislate a copyright for musical renditions, had not done so, thought the question of protection was left to the states. That New York favored protection could be inferred from lower-court decisions pushing the *I.N.S.* theme, notably the *Metropolitan Opera* decision of 1950.[33] Strictly, *I.N.S.* was now a stray, at most a pre-*Erie* declaration of national common law, but it was a handy citation for state judges around the country responding sporadically to an urge to prevent "reaping" or otherwise to prettify competition[34]—an urge which Professor Brown of Yale has likened, for nagging persistence, to the Manichaean Heresy.

Holding for the plaintiff, the majority of the Second Circuit Court of Appeals was just as oblivious to possible inferences arising from the Copyright Act as the state courts had been. Most peculiar is the fact that Judge Hand did not mention the point in his dissent[35]—for he was driven to dissent. One need not take the high road and say that the Copyright Act was a complete charter repelling recognition of a monopoly in a production outside the act. One could take the low road and consider whether a performer's right would be consistent with the specific provisions of the statute bearing on music. Let me interpose that I, in fact, later did attempt such an analysis and found that certain aspects of a full-blown performer's right might well collide with the statute.[36] Judge Hand's dissent

[33]Metropolitan Opera Ass'n, Inc. v. Wagner-Nichols Recorder Corp., 199 Misc. 786, 101 N.Y.S.2d 483 (Sup. Ct. 1950), *aff'd per curiam,* 279 App. Div. 632, 107 N.Y.S.2d 795 (1951).

[34]*Cf. Developments in the Law—Competitive Torts,* 77 HARV. L. REV. 888, 934-35 (1964).

[35]Compare Judge Hand's earlier decision in G. Ricordi & Co. v. Haendler, 194 F.2d 914 (2d Cir. 1952).

[36]Kaplan, *Performer's Right and Copyright: The Capitol Records Case,* 69 HARV. L. REV. 409, 430-39 (1956).

took neither the high nor the low road. Rather he reached destination by the heroic tactic of falling back on the Constitution.

Considering a work not covered by the act but within the potential coverage of the constitutional clause, a state, according to Hand, could protect it to the stage of publication. The "overriding purpose" of the clause, however, quite apart from action or (I add) pregnant inaction by Congress, "was to grant only for 'limited Times' the untrammelled exploitation of an author's 'Writings.' Either he must be content with such circumscribed exploitation as does not constitute 'publication,' or he must eventually dedicate his 'work' to the public."[37] It followed from this that what was publication for the constitutional purpose was a federal question. A further reason, according to Hand, was that only thus could the policy of national "uniformity,"[38] inherent in the clause, be preserved against state discrepancies. And the renditions in *Capitol Records* must be held published by reason of their distribution and sale. By this reasoning, you will notice, Hand would bar state protection even for a limited time of published "Writings" not covered by the Copyright Act. The policy of national uniformity would defeat the state protection, even if the policy of eventual dedication of published works was satisfied. This inhibition on the states Hand found in an implication, a negative one, from the Constitution—a far more serious business than raising a similar implication from a congressional statute.

The majority decision in *Capitol Records*, with its sunny

[37]L. Hand, C.J., dissenting in Capitol Records, Inc. v. Mercury Records Corp., 221 F.2d 657, 667 (2d Cir. 1955).
[38]*Ibid.*

prospect of a broad resort to state law, naturally elated the Manichaeans. They actually began to dream of a return to *Millar v. Taylor*, the old English case decided in 1769,[39] and later overruled by the *Donaldson* case,[40] which had viewed the whole statutory copyright as merely accumulative to sweeping common-law rights of perpetual extension. The dream is as vain as it is durable. But Judge Hand's dissent might be thought to go a bit too far in the opposite direction. For myself, I was led from some exegetical questions about the dissent to the perhaps unadventurous hypothesis that in its relation to state power the copyright clause might be not much different from, say, the commerce clause.[41] A regulation by an individual state might be so offensive to the intrinsic purpose of the copyright power as to be invalid even if Congress had not so much as tiptoed into the field of regulation: in this sense the clause would operate of its own force to invalidate the state law. A less egregious state regulation could stand unless inconsistent with a congressional enactment. With this attitude toward the cosmology of the copyright power, we would have to raise a doubt whether Judge Hand had not been too absolutist or doctrinaire in excluding state power. We would be entitled to play more of a waiting game.

I hope you are now eager for a message from the Supreme Court about *Capitol Records* and all that. A message has come—not altogether clear, but emphatic.

Some specialists thought they could see in *Capitol Records* a paradigm of liability under state law for various kinds of

[39]4 Burr. 2303, 98 Eng. Rep. 201 (K.B. 1769).
[40]Donaldson v. Becket, 2 Bro. P.C. 129, 1 Eng. Rep. 837, 4 Burr. 2408, 98 Eng. Rep. 257 (H.L. 1774). See *supra* pp. 14-15.
[41]See Kaplan, *supra* note 36, at 420-25.

attempted "free rides" not involving infringement of patent or copyright, or traditional palming off, or confusion of source.[42] Suppose, then, that a plaintiff secures a design patent for the configuration of his lamp fixtures and sues for patent infringement and also on the ground of "unfair competition" according to state law. The design patent fails, but the trial court enjoins the defendant from further manufacture on the second ground. Two cases on such facts, the *Sears*[43] and *Compco*[44] cases, reached the Supreme Court in 1964; the difference between them was that in the one there could hardly have been a pretense that anyone buying the defendant's fixture would think he was buying the plaintiff's, whereas in the other there was some proof of confusion—the configuration tended to point to the plaintiff as the source. The Supreme Court reversed and dismissed both actions. Here is some arresting and vital language from Justice Black's opinion in *Compco*: "when an article is unprotected by a patent or a copyright, state law may not forbid others to copy that article. To forbid copying would interfere with the federal policy, found in Art. I, § 8, cl. 8, of the Constitution and in the implementing federal statutes, of allowing free access to copy whatever the federal patent and copyright laws leave in the public domain. And further: "That an article copied from an unpatented article could be made in some other way, that the design is 'nonfunctional' and not essential to the use of either article, that the configuration of the article copied may have a 'secondary meaning' which identifies the maker to the trade,

---

[42]See Derenberg, *The Eighth Year of Administration of the Lanham Trademark Act of 1946*, 45 TRADEMARK REP. 987, 1048-49 (1955).
[43]Sears, Roebuck & Co. v. Stiffel Co., 376 U.S. 225 (1964).
[44]Compco Corp. v. Day-Brite Lighting, Inc., 376 U.S. 234 (1964).

or that there may be 'confusion' among purchasers as to which article is which or as to who is the maker, may be relevant evidence in applying a State's law requiring such precautions as labeling; however, and regardless of the copier's motives, neither these facts nor any others can furnish a basis for imposing liability for or prohibiting the actual acts of copying and selling."[45]

Something drastic seemed to have happened and the *Columbia Law Review* tried by means of a symposium to find out just what it was.[46] Commissioner Daphne Leeds wrote grimly that nothing much had happened; but she was barely holding back the tears. Professor Handler admitted much apparent damage to established state doctrines, and, in a magisterial mood, asked why Brandeis's plea in the *I.N.S.* dissent for judicial restraint in creating new law did not carry over to destroying old law. Professor Derenberg like a good lawyer immediately hatched plans for escaping the decisions. One could see Professor Brown taking long and easy strokes as he swam cheerfully in the wave of the future. Professor Bender in doleful analytic numbers chided the Court for its failure to give a fully reasoned explanation of what it was doing.

The Supreme Court has certainly come out against efforts by the states to quell copying as such. It also seems to have put the kibosh on the respectable if often abused doctrine that copying the appearance of a competing article, though in itself lawful, may within certain limits be forbidden in order to prevent confusion of source. In this overturn, in the diffi-

---

[45]*Id.* at 237, 238.
[46]Leeds, Handler, Derenberg, Brown & Bender, *Product Simulation: A Right or a Wrong?*, 64 COLUM. L. REV. 1178 (1964).

culty of divining how far the intended "preemption" of state law is based on the Constitution, how far on the monopoly statutes, and in the ultimate quandary about the exact reach of the preemption, the *Sears* and *Compco* cases have been disturbing to those of settled or tidy mind. In a general sense the Supreme Court has condemned accumulative state protection as the House of Lords in the *Donaldson* case forbade accumulative common-law protection; and deeply embedded in Justice Black's opinions is a conception of patent and copyright as singular exceptions to a pervasive and dominating rule of competition, which rests on imitation.[47] But, descending to particulars, has the Court spoken inferentially about such a case as *Capitol Records* where the work, the musical rendition, is a case not covered by the statute, rather than a case covered as to type but failing to qualify, as were the configurations in *Sears* and *Compco*? This is not clear, though we do find some Hand-like stress on national uniformity and on the iniquities of protection unlimited in time. Would the Court today condone a practice like that of I.N.S. on condition only that I.N.S. "label" its dispatches, tell the truth about their origin?[48] To return to the point or place of beginning, would the Court which decided the *Sears* and *Compco* cases be prepared to upset *Ferris v. Frohman* and work out a definition

[47] See also Black, J., in Aro Mfg. Co., Inc. v. Convertible Top Replacement Co., Inc., 377 U.S. 476, 522 (1964) (dissenting opinion).

[48] Holmes, J., took just this view in the I.N.S. case, 248 U.S. at 248. *But cf.* Pottstown Daily News Pub. Co. v. Pottstown Broadcasting Co., 411 Pa. 383, 192 A.2d 657 (1963); 247 F. Supp. 578 (E.D.Pa. 1965).

It is interesting to consider the effect of the Sears and Compco cases on another standby, Fisher v. Star Co., 231 N.Y. 414, 132 N.E. 133, *cert. denied,* 257 U.S. 654 (1921) (originator of "Mutt and Jeff" protected without regard to copyright status of his cartoons).

of publication that would avoid the reproach that it cheats the public domain?[49]

My discussion has been abstruse, but it comes down to this. A hugger-mugger over the concept of "publication" beginning a half-century ago has generated interesting possibilities of evading the controls of the Copyright Act even as to subject matter plainly within its reach. False classification of a copyright problem as being something different from that can have the same effect of evasion. As to subject matter not admitted to copyright by the present act, we have a turbulent condition of the law. And over the scene sound the oracular words of the Supreme Court, which must chill the blood of any dues-paying Manichaean.

The aberrant drive toward irregular protection is in part explained, no doubt, by inadequacies of our superannuated copyright statute. A revised law ought to wield a big broom, starting with a clean sweep of the "publication" crisis. One solution for publication would be to redefine it to include public dissemination by performance or similar exploitation, and this is attractive as long as one is thinking of a copyright period measured by years in gross, which needs some specific starting point. The blush fades from this peach when, as has recently happened, sentiment swings over to a "life-plus"

[49]At the same time as state law is being tested in the light of federal power and federal enactments regarding patent and copyright (see, among many cases, Cable Vision, Inc. v. KUTV, Inc., 335 F.2d 248 [9th Cir. 1964], *cert. denied*, 379 U.S. 989 [1965]), we find an effort to work out a sensible pattern of relationships among the federal patent, copyright, and trademark statutes. For just as state "unfair competition" doctrine may offend against federal patent or copyright policy, so may a too generous reading of the federal trademark statute. *Cf. The Supreme Court, 1963 Term*, 78 HARV. L. REV. 143, 311 (1964).

period of protection. That choice influences others, in domino style, and the Revision Bill has wound up with basic provisions about the subject matter of copyright, duration, and "preemption" as follows. Copyright, attaching to "works of authorship" which are "original" and "fixed in any tangible medium of expression,"[50] would subsist from the "creation" of the work and endure for the lifetime of a natural author plus 50 years.[51] The works comprise seven categories including, by the way, sound recordings, which are granted a qualified copyright.[52] "[A]ll rights in the nature of copyright" as to works within the Bill would be "governed exclusively" by it, and correspondingly no person would be entitled to such rights in those works "under the common law or statutes of any State."[53]

This general recipe, pushing the inception of federal copyright well back of publication and extruding state law, responds reasonably, I think, to the current problems both legal and practical. Some questions remain under the Bill that can be seen only in a half light.

(A) The draftsman evidently believed that the copyright clause, in speaking of "Writings," confines the federal power to works that are "fixed."[54] I should rather think the copyright

[50]Revision Bill §102.
[51]Revision Bill §302(a).
[52]Revision Bill §102(1)-(7). The list expressly includes "pantomimes and choreographic works," which must today claim any performing rights under the caption of "dramatic or dramatico-musical compositions." 17 U.S.C. §5(d) (1964).
[53]Revision Bill §301(a).
[54]See REGISTER OF COPYRIGHTS, COPYRIGHT LAW REVISION, REPORT ON THE GENERAL REVISION OF THE U.S. COPYRIGHT LAW, printed for the use of the House Committee on the Judiciary, 87th Cong., 1st Sess., at 9 (Comm. Print 1961).

power supplemented by the "necessary and proper" clause permits federal regulation of a work anticipating its fixation. But the remission of works, before they are fixed, to state regulation is not immediately embarrassing;[55] it might become so through technological changes at present unforeseeable, or a corruption of the idea of fixation to allow indefinite prolongation of rights, as "publication" was corrupted by the rule of *Ferris v. Frohman*.

(B) The provision against accumulative state protection to works under federal copyright is matched in the Bill by a saving section permitting state remedies for "activities violating rights that are not equivalent to any of the exclusive rights" within the scope of federal copyright, "including breaches of contract, breaches of trust, invasion of privacy, defamation, and deceptive trade practices such as passing off and false representation."[56] The strophe and antistrophe acknowledge generally, but rather imperfectly, that *Sears* and *Compco* have tuned their lyre. But if the Bill is to recite here what is left to state development, what about a distinct saver acknowledging state power to experiment with rights comparable to the Continental "moral rights"?[57]

(C) By still another provision, the Bill appears to admit state law for the regulation of any kinds of works remaining after one subtracts the works made subjects of copyright by the Bill from those constitutionally capable of copyright.[58]

---

[55]But see the peculiar technical problem that might arise under the Revision Bill if a live broadcast were pirated from the air at the very moment it was being "fixed" on tape. *House Hearings*, Pt. 2, at 1229; Pt. 3, at 1825-26, 1843-44, 1848-49.

[56]Revision Bill § 301(b)(3).

[57]See *supra* p. 78, n. 116.

[58]Revision Bill § 301(b)(1); and see § 101 (definition of "publication").

State power, however, is here confined to the stage before publication, defined for purposes of the Revision Bill in the sense of distribution to the public of the material objects in which works are embodied—we are reminded of Judge Hand's general position in *Capitol Records*. But what does the category consist of? I can hardly form a picture of it. Both the Bill and the commentary by the Register of Copyrights[59] are obscure. I gather it may include so commonplace a thing as a so-called "typographical" work, an original typographical arrangement. But I suppose it could also be taken to extend to now unimaginable technological advances—radical new ways of stimulating sight, hearing, or touch; perhaps new kinds of works bringing signals to other senses. Why, then, draw a line only at publication? But again the question merges in the larger issue, how far the legislation should try to deal with possible future developments by present dispositive rules.

As to the ascription and modulation of rights under a rule of live and let live—the third big task of revision—the Bill starts with a vesting of fivefold exclusive rights, including for the first time a measured statement of a right of public exhibition (in the sense of display); then follow crisscrossing limitations or exemptions, from a provision accepting broadly the doctrine of "fair use," down to a number of narrow particulars.[60] In these sections we find proposed settlements of those disputes between "producers" and "users" for which the Register has long been seeking reconciliation, or, as we now say, "consensus." Before reaching the battlegrounds, however, we should ask whether in the rights provisions any new light is

[59]COPYRIGHT LAW REVISION, PT. 6, at 3.
[60]Revision Bill §§ 106-14.

shed on the old question, "wherein consists the identity of a work," on the fundamental issues of copyrightability and infringement discussed in the second lecture. Very little light, if any; though I should mention that the definition of "derivative work" appearing in the Revision Bill has a most expansive look.[61] The enduring questions, then, the Bill allows the courts to pursue unaided; and this was to be expected.

With regard to the rights catalogued in the Bill, the Register's basic attitude is that they not only should be stated in broad terms, with a burden on any limitation to justify itself, but should aim to cover possible future as well as present utilizations.[62] This is in contrast to the Register's view that Congress should have a square look before admitting particular new subject matter to federal copyright. Thus the Revision Bill itself tenders to Congress the question of sound recordings as a new subject of copyright. And the draftsman asserts, as we have seen, that the Bill does not exhaust the subjects

[61]"A 'derivative work' is a work based upon one or more pre-existing works, such as a translation, musical arrangement, dramatization, fictionalization, motion picture version, sound recording, art reproduction, abridgment, condensation, or any other form in which a work may be recast, transformed, or adapted. A work consisting of editorial revisions, annotations, elaborations, or other modifications which, as a whole, represent an original work of authorship, is a 'derivative work.'" Revision Bill, § 101; see § 106 (a)(2).

Certain influential groups have made the extraordinary suggestion that the right of the proprietor of a copyrighted work should also extend to the making of a "supplementary work," which they would define as "a work prepared for publication as a secondary adjunct to a work by another author for the purpose of introducing, concluding, illustrating, explaining, revising, commenting upon or assisting in the use of the other work, such as forewords, introductions, prefaces, prologues, epilogues, illustrations, musical arrangements, maps, charts, tables, editorial notes, tests, bibliographies, appendixes, and indexes." *House Hearings*, Pt. 1, at 134, under §§ 101, 106. See also *supra* p. 58, n. 57.

[62]See COPYRIGHT LAW REVISION, PT. 6, at 13-14.

copyrightable under the Constitution: if additional subjects are hereafter to get federal protection, Congress will have to act. The explanation of the more protective attitude toward emergent and future uses, an attitude I find somewhat troublesome, lies in the Register's searing experience with jukeboxes. Back in 1909 the lawmakers lightheartedly exempted performance of music on coin-operated machines from any copyright toll unless a fee was charged for admission to the place of entertainment.[63] Such machines were then thought of as unpromising toys. Some toys! It has proved impossible to dislodge the exemption—which the Revision Bill again, and in my view correctly, seeks to remove—because a lobby has stood guard over every word and comma. But let me get to the meat and comment briefly on a few of the attempts in the Bill to settle producer-user quarrels by combining a certain amount of compromise with a certain amount of foresight.

Photocopying. Machine copying of texts is getting progressively easier and cheaper; and it can be done privately, without attracting much attention to itself. Scholars, teachers, and librarians of course insist on this copying as essential to their work. It is a question whether publishers and, back of them, authors have as yet been deprived of any substantial amount of business that they could have managed for themselves, but a big potential for injury does exist: photocopying *ad lib.* could not only deprive publishers and authors of a return from these burgeoning uses amounting to a new market but also damage their existing market. *Hinc illae lacrimae.* What photocopying is at present lawful is a little in doubt. The supposition that there is no tort involved in a scholar copying a copyrighted

[63]Copyright Act of 1909, § 1(e), now 17 U.S.C. § 1(e) (1964).

text by hand does not much advance the question of machine copying, precisely because the commercial threat is greater. Does it make any difference that the text is out of print or that only a part is being copied? A proposal for a specific and rather moderate exemption for photocopying by public libraries was rejected by both sides. Also rejected was a proposed statutory elucidation of fair use, intended to provide some help on photocopying.[64] The Revision Bill is reduced to uttering on the subject only the staccato bleat of just the words "fair use."[65] It seems hardly a statesmanlike result to leave a sizable fraction of the population (including, I fancy, some of those enjoying this lecture) thus uncertainly subject to civil and even criminal liability for acts now as habitual to them as a shave in the morning, especially as publishers are still far from devising any simple methods by which this public could calculate and make the payments that might clearly legitimate those habits. We do hear talk of creating some ASCAP-like system, but at present it is only talk. Of course the problem called "photocopying" actually extends to a much larger "reprographic" technology; and we must not forget the new home device for copying television broadcasts, behind which loom still other machines.

Computers. Here the draftsman first vainly attempted an answer in the form of a single special clause.[66] The problem is now being consigned largely to the general language of the

---

[64]"Preliminary draft," § 7, and revision bill of 1964, § 6, both appearing in COPYRIGHT LAW REVISION, PT. 6, at 193.

[65]Revision Bill § 107.

[66]"Preliminary draft," § 5(a), in COPYRIGHT LAW REVISION, PT. 6, at 187.

Revision Bill about reproduction and so forth.[67] This solution is neither clear nor bland.

First, as to computer "programs" (in the sense of instructions to the machine). Under the Bill an original program, whether on punch cards, tapes, or what not, would be itself copyrightable, and that sounds right;[68] but the question is promptly raised, and left dangling, how far the copyright would or should extend to practical utilization of the program. This begins to look like a revival of the problem of *Baker v. Selden*[69] —the old case holding that copyright of books describing a bookkeeping method conferred no monopoly of the method. I can give only a hint of further difficulties. What is the meaning of infringement here? Take a program written with knowledge of a copyrighted program and attaining a similar result by different steps or sequences of steps. A suspicion, indeed, that we ought to be thinking not copyright but patent or perhaps a third quiddity, arises as we are told that the programs, or some of them, can be translated, so to speak, into physical parts of the computer's machinery or circuitry.[70]

Second, as to uses or manipulations of copyrighted material by the computer. The Register thinks that copying a copyrighted work for storage in the machine should itself be an

[67]See Revision Bill §§ 101 (definitions of "copies" and "literary works"), 102, 106(a)(1), (5).

[68]See Copyright Office Circular 31D (January 1965), setting forth terms on which the Office will accept computer programs for registration under the present statute.

[69]101 U.S. 99 (1879); see *supra* pp. 33, 63-66.

[70]The Patent Office has just published and invited comments on tentative "Guidelines" which it proposes to adopt for examination of applications for patent on "programming methods and apparatus." 829 OFFICIAL GAZETTE OF U.S. PATENT OFF., No. 1, at 1 (2 August 1966).

infringement if unlicensed.[71] But should not infringement turn on what is subsequently done with the stored work? Printouts of the work would be analogous to photocopies, but suppose the printout is merely an index or short résumé taking nothing substantial from the work; suppose the work is merely exhibited by the machine to its clients in circumstances which would otherwise constitute an exempt occasion? The Register evidently believes copying for storage must be controlled because the machines are capable of a great variety of uses and outputs, but it is not apparent to me that the Register's blanket proposal is prudent at the present stage of computer development or sound for the long future.

CATV. Ever since the invention of radio there has been a nice question "where, if anywhere, in a chain of transmissions and public reception, the copyright owner's control should stop."[72] Today the problem extends to images as well as sounds and has been much exacerbated. The Revision Bill performs the nerve-wracking job of distinguishing a radio turned on by the proprietor of a barbershop (which it proposes to rule innocent), from the same instrument turned on and boosted by the owner of a supermarket (guilty), and that in turn from a radio in a hotel whose sound is wired to the private rooms (innocent). I think the Register also wants to exculpate a landlord who installs a special antenna for his tenants to bring in otherwise unreachable signals.[73] Is there a tenable difference between the hotel and landlord cases, on the one hand, and,

[71]COPYRIGHT LAW REVISION, PT. 6, at 18.
[72]COPYRIGHT LAW REVISION, PT. 6, at 40.
[73]See Revision Bill §§ 109(5)-(7) and discussion in COPYRIGHT LAW REVISION, PT. 6, at 40-44. With respect to the hotel case, the Bill would overrule the decision in Buck v. Jewell-LaSalle Realty Co., 283 U.S. 191 (1931) (opinion by Brandeis, J.).

on the other, a for-profit "community antenna" system typically consisting, as the Register describes it, of a "central antenna which receives and amplifies television signals, and a network of cables through which the signals are then transmitted to the receiving sets of individual subscribers who thereby get better reception and more channels to choose from"?[74] The Revision Bill comes down against the CATV relay as an infringing transmission.[75] If the criterion here is "transmission" in some peculiar physical sense, then the decision can of course be rationalized.[76] But what impresses itself on a reader of the reciprocally harsh propaganda about CATV is the inappositeness or rather the incompleteness of such a criterion and the thinness of any analysis based upon it. In a deeper view the copyright question is seen as but one phase of the problem of the place of CATV systems in national communications. In February 1966 the FCC completed a 180-degree turn of policy and announced its assumption of broad regulatory authority

[74]COPYRIGHT LAW REVISION, PT. 6, at 40.

[75]See COPYRIGHT LAW REVISION, PT. 6, at 40-43; cf. Revision Bill § 109(5).

[76]It was essentially by reference to such a criterion that Judge Herlands on 23 May 1966 held a CATV system, using the signal of a station broadcasting copyrighted motion pictures, to be infringing the copyright of the pictures, more particularly the performance rights under present law, 17 U.S.C. §§ 1(c), (d) (1964). United Artists Television, Inc. v. Fortnightly Corp., 149 U.S.P.Q. 758 (S.D.N.Y. 1966). This decision has been appealed pursuant to leave of the Court of Appeals and is pending argument there. Cf. Columbia Broadcasting System v. Teleprompter Corp., 148 U.S.P.Q. 417 (S.D.N.Y. 1965) (similar action; issues held too complex to be decided on motion for summary judgment).

For the abortive efforts to hold CATV systems liable for "unfair competition," see Intermountain Broadcasting & Television Corp v. Idaho Microwave, Inc., 196 F. Supp. 315 (S.D.Idaho 1961); Cable Vision, Inc. v. KUTV, Inc., 335 F.2d 348 (9th Cir. 1964), cert. denied, 379 U.S. 989 (1965), rev'g 211 F. Supp. 47 (S.D.Idaho 1962) (reversal based on the Sears and Compco decisions).

over CATV.[77] This should be taken, I think, to vacate the Register's proposal in the Revision Bill and to invite a reassessment of it.[78] Instead of conjuring with "transmission," we have to consider whether clamping down copyright controls would have any hurtful anticompetitive effects or would be consistent with the declared purposes of the Federal Communications Act or would serve as a desirable means of correcting the hardships which CATV systems may visit on TV stations in the same localities.[79]

Various educational uses. Educators pay a very large toll annually to copyright proprietors; but in certain respects, as nonprofit users, they have long been favored by copyright doctrine and legislation, and they have long acted as though they were entitled to other favors that are perhaps not so clear under the law. Having already mentioned photocopying, I

[77]Public Notice, Regulation of CATV Systems, 6 Pike & Fischer Radio Reg. 2d 1637 (15 February 1966), followed by Second Report and Order, 6 *id.* at 1717 (8 March 1966).

[78]In its Second Report and Order, *supra* note 77, the FCC noted that the rules therein set forth might have to be revised if the pending copyright suits against CATV systems were decided adversely to CATV. See 6 *id.* at 1770.

[79]In a statement of 25 August 1966 presented to the Senate subcommittee, *supra* note 1, the Justice Department through Assistant Attorney General Zimmerman expressed opposition to the Revision Bill's treatment of CATV. In the Department's view, the CATV problem would be better handled "through flexible regulation by the FCC uninhibited by a blanket copyright liability." If this view is not followed, the Department believes that "copyright revision should at least take account of communications policy and distinguish between different CATV operations for the purpose of copyright liability."
On 5 May 1966 the House subcommittee, *supra* note 1, had declared its intention to recommend to the full committee detailed amendments of the Revision Bill which would exempt certain CATV operations from copyright liability, subject other operations to full copyright sanctions, and permit still others on payment of reasonable fees on a compulsory license basis. See 112 Cong. Rec. 9564 (daily ed. 9 May 1966).

shall not touch the question of multiplication of tangible copies of works for teaching purposes, except to say that the fact of an educational, nonprofit motive is generally considered to work towards excuse from liability in the sense of fair use. Here the Revision Bill would leave particular interpretations to the courts, as we have seen. The Bill attempts to be more precise as to other uses, and I shall take a few illustrations. The present statute exempts the public performance of nondramatic literary or musical works if it is not for profit; but the proprietor's performance right in dramatic works extends to public performance even if not for profit.[80] Under these arrangements, a great many educational uses are free of copyright accountability. Now, impressed by the sheer spread of educational uses, the Register thinks education should devote more of its money—always and inevitably in short supply—to compensating copyright owners; he is no longer satisfied with the simple statutory lines. The result in the Revision Bill is specific exemptions in lieu of the general. There would be an exemption for the performance or exhibition of any works in face-to-face nonprofit teaching activities, but beware too strong a recreational element or, possibly, having a lot of parents in the room at the time.[81] Performance of nondramatic literary or musical works or exhibition of works, by transmission, as part of the systematic, nonprofit instruction of students, would be allowable within certain limits; but much of the programming of educational broadcasting stations would lose its existing exempt status.[82] Now it is no wonder that teachers and others who would be deprived by the new detailed code of some existing

[80]17 U.S.C. §§ 1(c)-(e) (1964).
[81]Revision Bill § 109(1); COPYRIGHT LAW REVISION, PT. 6, at 32-34.
[82]Revision Bill § 109(2); COPYRIGHT LAW REVISION, PT. 6, at 34-37.

benefit are making loud moan; at the same time publishers
claim to see their own eventual extinction in the encouragement given to the use of devices which can make one tangible
copy serve in place of many. It is hard to know where the
ideal line of exemption should run; the Register's line, being
nervous and finical, would probably begin to irk very soon.
However, the notion held by some publishers, that the preferment of educational users springs entirely from sentiment,
not reason, seems to me wrong. It is wrong if we posit that
copyright seeks an optimum combination of producer's incentive with users' benefits: that will justify preferment under
conditions which can be generally described. At a certain
point, no doubt, exact reason fails; and here I would join in
the Register's call to all those here embattled to recognize that
authorship, publishing, education, and research are interde-
pendent and mutually supportive endeavors.

Sound recordings. Once the copyright proprietor of a nondramatic musical composition has made or authorized another
to make phonorecords of the music, anyone else becomes entitled to make records of the composition on payment of "two-
cents-a-side" (of course the parties remain free to negotiate a
lesser fee). This is the "compulsory license" introduced in the
1909 act after the decision in the *White-Smith* case[83] about
music rolls. The license provision was intended—so it has been
commonly supposed—to meet a threat of monopolization of the
market by one company. That specific threat receded. Yet, to
the consternation of economists, the two-cent license provision
still abides with us. After first recommending repeal of the
license, the Register has now come around simply to marking

[83]White-Smith Music Pub. Co. v. Apollo Co., 209 U.S. 1 (1908);
Copyright Act of 1909, § 1(e), now 17 U.S.C. § 1(e) (1964).

the figure up to three cents.[84] I do not shrink, as some do, from
the idea of a compulsory license, but enacting a specific rate to
last indefinitely seems odd, notwithstanding the fact that the
industry has long been used to living with one; and I have
not seen a convincing case even under present conditions for
the precise markup proposed.[85]

The Revision Bill also intends for the first time to accord
copyright of a sort to sound recordings distinct from the notational compositions. (Shades of the *Whiteman* and *Capitol
Records* cases.) Truly astonishing has been the vehemence of
the dispute over the shape of this copyright and who is to
control it. In the end a public performance right was withheld;
the right granted would be that of preventing "dubbing,"
inscribing the very sounds on other phonorecords.[86] On the
question of control, the Revision Bill takes the ostrich tack
of omitting to say who is to be the presumptive owner of the
copyright—performer, manufacturer, or both.

I now sum up on the solutions for the producer-user issues
that are proffered by the Revision Bill. Their trend seems
toward enlargement or enhancement of monopoly rights; and
enforcement remedies would also be sharpened in sections of
the Bill that I shall not describe. Certain of the solutions turn
out to be mere remissions of the problems to the courts al-

[84]Revision Bill § 113(c)(2); cf. 1961 Report, *supra* note 54, at 32-36.
[85]To prevent use of the compulsory license as a means of legalizing
"distortions or travesties" of the copyrighted composition (see COPYRIGHT
LAW REVISION, PT. 6, at 55), Revision Bill § 113(a)(2) provides that the
licensee's arrangement of the composition "shall not change the basic
melody or fundamental character of the work." I doubt the workability or
wisdom of this provision, and question how it is intended to connect with
the "fair use" provision of § 107. Cf. *supra* p. 69.
[86]Revision Bill § 112.

though firmer answers would be desirable if feasible. Other solutions are indeed firm, but it appears that a change of perspective or a shift of technology would show them up as very wrong or very foolish. Consider the computer, keeping in mind that the art itself is unstable.

I am aware that the Bill as now drawn is not the last word. Negotiations continue, and better results may come by dint of still more talk or through the clash of power with countervailing power. The general problem for the near future is after all a happy one, that of dealing with a rapidly expanding market for copyrighted works—and it is not impertinent to remind the contestants that this condition has been largely brought about by independent scientific invention owing little to any of the copyright factions.

In the interest of temperate solutions it will be well to stress the Register's own suggestion that broad rights can be moderated by withholding drastic sanctions such as the injunction or (what may amount to the same thing) by introducing a compulsory license.[87] So also the rights vested in the copyright proprietor can be reduced in scope or number, or exemptions enlarged or added, as the work grows older. But even after the utmost efforts at optimal legislative answers on these or other lines, there will remain a danger of freezing into permanent law provisions unduly indefinite or merely adventitious or wildly anticipatory. The jukebox story shows how entrenched a statutory exemption can become, but the same can happen to a statute-granted right. It is natural, therefore—although quite alien to the outlook of many of the specialist Bar—to consider leavening the Bill with a delegated administrative

[87]Testimony of the Register, 2 September 1965, in *House Hearings*, Pt. 3, at 1859.

power that could within stated limits adapt the statute to changing realities, realities that must be studied continuously, and to which bare, occasional congressional responses are apt to be late or inadequate.[88] Some of the authority would have to be vested in a board or commission, rather than confided to the Register alone; important exercises might have to rise as high as the President; waiting periods would perhaps have to be allowed for congressional negatives. I conceive of the authority as going not merely to modifications of the dubious equilibriums that will be attained in the statute between producers and users but as extending to other matters, for example, recasting the formalities, eventually admitting new subject matter to the copyright system, assisting in the management of compulsory licenses if any are imposed by the statute, and in the creation and development of the ASCAP-like structures already mentioned. The administrative expedient is one that we can come to only with regret and some misgiving: for it would do away with the simplicity, one may even say the pristine innocence, of copyright law. Yes, I can imagine plenty of sensible objections to the idea, and more to the details; but I would not count among them the broad contention that a mere commission should not be put in a position to shift substantial values from one industrial group to another, as the copyright commission would have to be empowered to do here.

The problem of the duration of copyright forms a coda to the question of the rights to be accorded to the copyright pro-

[88]Professor Chafee wrote of such a possibility a generation ago, *Reflections on the Law of Copyright: II*, 45 COLUM. L. REV. 719, 737-38 (1945), and for at least one kind of future contingency Professor Nimmer reached for the same device in his testimony, 26 August 1965, in *House Hearings*, Pt. 3, at 1815-16.

prietor. We now have a term of twenty-eight years, with a
second term of twenty-eight years if renewal registration is
made in the last year of the initial period.[89] Why a renewal
feature? First, to enrich the public domain with works that
will not be re-registered because they have no continuing commercial value, though they may have continuing cultural interest. Second, the renewal was thought of as a way of protecting
a natural author against his own improvidence in assigning or
licensing the copyright. The idea was to have the renewal
revert to the author free and clear, so that it might be traded
with afresh on perhaps better terms. This sounds easy but is
in fact tough to work out: a complicating factor is death of
the author. The present statutory provision, as interpreted, is
a goulash. Suppose the author in the first year of copyright
purports to sell it—both the initial and renewal terms. The
effect of the *Fred Fisher* case[90] and other authorities is that
if the author is dead when the twenty-eighth year comes
round, the renewal reverts, free and clear, to his widow,
children, and so forth in a fixed order of precedency; but if
the author is alive in that year, the original sale holds and there
is no reversion. The distinction is hard to defend and may
operate in a peculiarly perverse way where on the faith of a
transfer from the now-deceased author, the transferee has
created a "derivative work," say a movie based on the original
novel.

With widespread agreement that the present system is
wrong, the Register in the Revision Bill has abandoned the
system of a renewable term and has opted for a single term of

[89] 17 U.S.C. § 24 (1964).
[90] Fred Fisher Music Co. v. M. Witmark & Sons, 318 U.S. 643 (1943).

life plus fifty years.[91] Statistically analyzed, this is equivalent
to a period in gross of about seventy-six years. The Register
tries to explain the twenty-year enlargement of the length of
copyright by pointing to the fact that some works—to be sure,
a very small number—have commercial lasting power beyond
the fifty-six years now allowed and while the author or his near
relatives may be still alive; the Register has also been impressed by the fact that many foreign countries have adopted
the life-plus-fifty formula.[92] But, having justified the proposed
longer term as being for the benefit of the author and his
dependents, the Register cast about for some corrective for
long-term transfers by authors. This emerges in the Bill in the
form of a power in the author or his widow and children, at
his or their election, to terminate any transfer the author has
made after it has run thirty-five years, saving, however, the
right of a transferee to continue to utilize any derivative work
he has prepared during that period under authority of the
transfer.[93] It is hard to put the recapture idea in viable form.[94]
I have been talking so far about the works of "natural" authors.
As to "works made for hire," that is, works prepared by employees with copyright vesting in the employer from the
beginning, a category taking in today about four out of every
ten registered works, copyright would run for seventy-five

[91]Revision Bill § 302.
[92]COPYRIGHT LAW REVISION, PT. 6, at 86-88.
[93]Revision Bill § 203.
[94]I have gradually become more optimistic about working this problem
out, but proposed § 203 remains troublesome. Among the questions are
whether the power of recapture should arise so late in the copyright term,
whether recapture by the author or his successors should be wholly excluded
as to "works for hire" as now defined by the Bill, and whether the power,
when held by more than one individual, should be capable of exercise only
by unanimous vote, as the Bill now contemplates.

years from publication or one hundred years from creation, whichever period was shorter;[95] there would be no overriding power to terminate grants under the copyright. The extended term set for these "for-hire" works cannot be justified as benefiting natural authors or their dependents; the provision is more generous to the proprietor, I believe, than those found prevailingly in foreign countries going on a life-plus basis. Lastly, the Revision Bill makes no separate arrangement for archival material, that is, unpublished material held by libraries; duration of copyright would follow the rules stated.

I have reversed the classical order of exposition by discussing the question of duration of copyright after, rather than before, the nature and intensity of the rights conferred on the proprietor. It is evident that as rights are strengthened, they need run, and can be endured, only for a correspondingly shorter period. So, if copyright proprietors are given really comprehensive rights to prevent uses of their works in computers, it will, I am sure, ultimately become plain to everyone that the copyright period must be cut very short. My concern that the term of copyright proposed in the Revision Bill is too long is thus fed by the several other high-protectionist tendencies of the Bill, and I must finally say that I doubt a convincing case has been made for extending copyright in works of natural authors a generation's worth beyond the present statutory term; still less has a case been made for extension of the term of works made "for hire."

With the ordinary régime of the market modified by the addition of monopoly aids, an estimate of the inducements to producers calculated to maximize public satisfactions becomes

[95]Revision Bill § 302(c).

the chief rational measure of copyright protection: the term
of copyright figures among the inducements. I invoke here
the same principle of moderation, of civility, that I tried to
apply to questions of infringement in the second lecture. It is
the principle I extract from the debates of Macaulay and Talfourd, of Renouard and Lieber, from the writings of the
masters of all shades of opinion from Eaton Sylvester Drone
to Zechariah Chafee.[96] In a condition of society in which
nearly all else is moving and obsolescing at an accelerating
pace, in which businessmen are rarely moved by any but
quick-return prospects, it seems to me passing strange to be
now thinking of prolonging copyright. That scattered works
may have commercial value after fifty-six years hardly seems
a justification for keeping all works under wraps for another
twenty years. We ought to recognize clearly that any incre-
ment of benefit to the author and publisher achieved by prolonging the period of protection is quite soon outrun by the
burden imposed on others. The Register properly considers
greater agreement among the nations of the world on the term
of copyright to be a worthy and attractive goal, but the question remains, what term?

Passing from exploited works to inert archival material—
manuscripts, letters, and so on—the proposed term seems again
too long, although it is a considerable improvement on the

[96]1 MISCELLANIES BY LORD MACAULAY 234, 253 (1901) (speeches of 5
February 1841, 6 April 1842); TALFOURD, THREE SPEECHES DELIVERED
IN THE HOUSE OF COMMONS IN FAVOUR OF A MEASURE FOR AN EXTENSION
OF COPYRIGHT (1840); Renouard, *Theory of the Rights of Authors,* 22
AM. JUR. & LAW MAG. 39 (1840); 2 LIEBER, MISCELLANEOUS WRITINGS
329 (1881) (letter to William C. Preston, March 1840); DRONE, A
TREATISE ON THE LAW OF PROPERTY IN INTELLECTUAL PRODUCTIONS, esp.
49-53 (1879); Chafee, *Reflections on the Law of Copyright: I, II,* 45
COLUM. L. REV. 503, 719 (1945).

theoretically perpetual copyright now accorded by our law to unpublished works, which has often made the publication of old letters and like material nightmarishly difficult. I agree here with the American Council of Learned Societies. In urging a shorter term for archival papers, the Council has spoken of "an ever-increasing interest in scholarship on subjects of relatively more contemporaneous vintage," of the continual shortening of "acceptable periods for gestation of private writings" in the matrix of history and criticism, and the consequent desirability of encouraging by law "the dissemination of knowledge about relatively recent affairs based on available primary source materials."[97]

I am sadly aware that what I have said about the copyright term will cause pain to some of my old friends at the copyright Bar who may come to suspect that under my cloak of bonhomie I conceal the bomb of a revolutionary enemy of private property. Recently a professorial colleague was accused only half jestingly of being a far-out radical when he ventured the mild suggestion that the basic copyright period should be the author's life plus twenty-five years. Commuted to years in gross, the suggested period is about that in the present statute, and it might be thought difficult to find the hand of Karl Marx in the act of 1909. Shall I now say in candor that I have sometimes dared to think even the fifty-six years is too much?

If I doubt that any kind of work or right requires the term proposed in the Revision Bill, I am quite sure that certain kinds do not. With this observation I imagine the Register might agree, were it not for a feeling that administrative efficiency calls for the same term for all works. Injudicious discrimina-

[97] *House Hearings*, Pt. 3, at 1554.

tions among works or rights could surely be embarrassing, for modern artistic endeavor tends to mingle and mix its brew in an appeal to all the senses, and the falling in of several elements of a composition at different times should be avoided if possible. But I have grosser discriminations in mind and point to foreign experience in assigning varying terms to various kinds of works.[98]

Let us now regard the longer future. It is a discouraging fact (if it is a fact) that of all the conceivable futures, only one will come to pass. This makes prophesying a strenuous and hazardous business, and I do not propose to try much of it.

The cult of originality, mentioned in the first lecture as having reinforced ideas of individual ownership of artistic productions, continues strongly into the present, although the forces that sustain it have undergone much change. Are there influences at work that will in time abate feelings of proprietorship and thus modify conceptions of copyright, especially those bearing on plagiarism? Probably so.

Much intellectual work including the distinctively imaginative is now being done by teams, a practice apt to continue and grow. The French have a name for it—*travaux d'équipe*. Such collaboration, I fancy, may diffuse and diminish emotions of original discovery and exclusive ownership.[99] I suggest,

[98]*Cf.* Guinan, *Duration of Copyright*, Study No. 30 Prepared for the Subcommittee on Patents, Trademarks, and Copyright of the Senate Comm. on the Judiciary, 86th Cong., 2d Sess., at 79 (Comm. Print 1961); 1 LADAS, THE INTERNATIONAL PROTECTION OF LITERARY AND ARTISTIC PROPERTY 311-42 (1938).

[99]Parenthetically, the Revision Bill leaves untouched the common-law rules regarding the management and administration of "joint works" as among the owners, and as between them and others. The increasing rate of

further, that the introduction of machines into the very creative process—computer-made music and poetry are crude examples of this development—will affect attitudes throughout copyright, besides raising difficult questions about copyrightability and infringement of the particular works. With mutations of machines, already imaginable, that foreshadow symbiotic relationships with the human brain, ideas of individuality and personality in relation to intellectual accomplishment may themselves be shaken. Meanwhile Professor Overhage shows us that in full-scale "on-line" operations with computers, the distinction between the author or producer of stored material and the user of the material tends to be blurred.[100] One is reminded of "aleatoric" music in which the line between performer and composer wavers. Professor McLuhan, a professional soothsayer, says broadly that as the imperium in communications passes from books to electronic manifestations, as the "Gutenberg galaxy"[101] decays, not only is the relationship between author and audience radically changed but the author's pretensions to individual ownership and achievement are at a discount: his dependence on the past is better appreciated; he is seen somewhat as a tradition-bearing "singer of tales," as a kind of teacher peculiarly indebted to his teachers before him. (I suppose claims of exempt status for educational uses of copyrighted works dimly reflect such an idea.)

---

collaborative production may be expected to compel a reexamination of this branch of copyright law before long.

[100]INTREX: REPORT OF A PLANNING CONFERENCE ON INFORMATION TRANSFER EXPERIMENTS 29, 34-35 (Overhage & Harman eds. 1965).

[101]McLUHAN, THE GUTENBERG GALAXY: THE MAKING OF TYPOGRAPHIC MAN (1962).

But we must look more closely at the technological environment of copyright. Publishers, phonograph record manufacturers, play producers, broadcasters, all the picturesque folk of the communications family of today, will, I hope, remain visible for some time to come; but to survive they will have to adjust themselves to the changing cosmos. The scramble is indeed well under way. I need only recall the recent mergers of electronics companies with book publishers, mergers that join masters of the new projection techniques with traditional holders and acquirers of the intellectual matter to be projected. Such changes of methods and of industrial alignments, though unsettling, are as yet interstitial; but they may be signposts to a gaudier future that almost blinds the eye. Here is my own bedtime story or pipedream which you are at perfect liberty to disbelieve.

You must imagine, at the eventual heart of things to come, linked or integrated systems or networks of computers capable of storing faithful simulacra of the entire treasure of the accumulated knowledge and artistic production of past ages, and of taking into the store new intelligence of all sorts as produced. The systems will have a prodigious capacity for manipulating the store in useful ways, for selecting portions of it upon call and transmitting them to any distance, where they will be converted as desired to forms directly or indirectly cognizable, whether as printed pages, phonorecords, tapes, transient displays of sights or sounds, or hieroglyphs for further machine uses. Lasers, microwave channels, satellites improving on Comsat's Early Bird, and, no doubt, many devices now unnamable, will operate as ganglions to extend the reach of the systems to the ultimate users as well as to provide a copious array of additional services.

Conceived as conduits or highways for the transmission of signals, the systems will have intense responsibilities of a "public utility" type enforced by law—if indeed the systems (or some of them) will not come under direct government ownership and control. Horrors of Orwellian dimensions lurk in far-reaching official regulation of the communications pattern; but to say that is merely to sound a summons to wise public regulation. If the systems will have public duties, so will new intellectual productions once unbosomed and released by the authors—the duties of submitting themselves to deposit in some form appropriate for archival purposes and to permit any manipulations of indexing, abstracting, and so forth needed to connect them, to key them in, with the existing store. This contribution made by new works need not involve their exposure to full-length use by unwelcome clients. At present, self-interest on the part of authors and publishers has usually resulted in adequate public access to works, and the law has rarely had to become insistent. Probably the law of the future will lose patience rather quickly with the mere idiosyncratic withholding of access. But I should hope there will ever be play for the humane development of the "moral rights" of authors to prevent abuses in the exploitation of their creations. This will indeed be especially important if copyright itself recedes as a significant control.

Copyright is likely to recede, to lose relevance, in respect to most kinds of uses of a great amount of scholarly production which now sees light in a mélange of learned journals and in the output of university presses. In the future little of this will ever be published in conventional book or journal form. Authors will offer their manuscripts for editorial screening; upon acceptance the material will enter directly into the electronic system, where it will be open to quick retrieval for consultation and study. (One energetic mind has conceived that the cost of introducing works into a system may finally run so low as to justify inclusion, in earmarked "compart-ments," of works rejected by the editors: an authors' paradise!) For many of the uses available through the machine, exaction of copyright payments will be felt unnecessary to provide incentive or headstart—especially so, when the works owe their origin, as so many will, to one or another kind of public support.[102]

I am suggesting that copyright or the larger part of its controls will appear unneeded, merely obstructive, as applied to certain sectors of production and that here copyright law will lapse into disuse and may disappear. For the rest, copy-right will persist to serve its historic purposes. For various early, prime exploitations of particular new works, whether or not accomplished through the electronic systems, there will be individual accountings, with separate financial hazards and successes or failures. The secondary and later exploitations will be largely through the systems. The ingenuity which devises the systems will no doubt be capable of welding-in bookkeep-ing apparatus that can continue for the whole copyright period to bill the customers monthly or weekly with exact

[102]I should add here that for the present I do not object to Revision Bill § 105 which declares works of the United States Government uncopy-rightable, but defines such a work narrowly—"prepared by an officer or em-ployee of the United States Government within the scope of his official duties or employment"—thus permitting copyright of works produced un-der government contract or with government money. The realities and varieties of government contracting and subsidizing today seem to me to counsel against the adoption of a total prohibition on permitting govern-ment contractors or beneficiaries to take copyright, but I would hope for caution in the formulation of administrative policies in this regard.

copyright charges per work used, as well as with system tolls, and then to make precise royalty remittances to the copyright owners. Perhaps this ingenuity will also be equal to the task of preventing unconsented-to private copying of works by duplicating machines or compelling it to leave traces on the machines that can be followed up by some omnicompetent bookkeeper. But what is suggested, on more sober reflection, is methods by which large repertories of works will be made available for a great variety of uses, and charges and remittances figured on a rough-and-ready basis, all with liberal application of some principle of "clearance at the source" to prevent undue bother down the line to the final consumer.

Unless, indeed, the systems are set up by government direct, government will probably intervene to establish fair standards for admission of works into the systems, for giving potential users access to the systems, for figuring rates, for making distributions to copyright owners. But under conditions of extensive government concern with the operations of the systems, which will have become supremely facile and widely encompassing of the transmission of intelligence, it may appear sensible to displace copyright and substitute other, perhaps more direct, encouragements to original production. We may in any case expect legislators of the future to regard copyright as only one among a number of expedients for stimulating creativity.

Meanwhile we have to observe that the electronic systems need not, and probably will not, remain national; they will be linked, possibly with the aid of automatic translation, in world-wide networks. Already we have a kind of practical internationalization by means of Early Bird. Apparent, then, is the need for further unification or harmonization of national copyright laws under improved international aegis, to the end that works shall travel from one country to another with valid passports and receive reasonably similar and decent treatment in each. Neither the Universal Copyright Convention, which is today our major copyright bridge to the outer world, nor the older Berne Convention, to which we have fitfully aspired, attains the ideal.

Of course it would be folly to expect all the nations of the world, including the new ones, to introduce at the present stage the same copyright régime as we and other well-endowed old-timers are—or, in the case of the U.S.S.R., should be—willing to accept. We should recall that until 1891 this country, claiming to be a have-not, provided no legal protection whatever to the published works of foreigners. When our legislation of 1891 finally did grant rights to such works, it was on the condition, in the case of books among certain other productions, that manufacture be carried out in the United States.[103] This was the "manufacturing clause," whose descendant in the present copyright statute[104] constituted a stone of stumbling in the drafting of the U.C.C. and was finally and happily removed from the path of works qualifying under that convention.[105] The manufacturing clause, however, persists to bedevil, principally, the publication of English-language books and periodicals by United States authors or foreign authors outside U.C.C. shelter. I am convinced that the clause has lost all practical justification. It is seen from the outside as merely

[103]Act of 3 March 1891, ch. 565, § 3, 26 Stat. 1107, amending Rev. Stat. § 4956 (1875).
[104]17 U.S.C. §§ 16, 17, 22, 23, 107 (1964).
[105]17 U.S.C. § 9 (c) (1964).

a xenophobic trade barrier. It should be simply repealed, as
the Register first proposed; the substitute appearing in the
Revision Bill is more intelligent, more humane than the
present clause, but still offensive.[106] But I have brought in
the manufacturing clause to suggest by example that harmonization is bound to have its difficulties and, beyond that, to
propose that we ourselves should take another step toward
international pacification.

To recapitulate, and close: In lecture one, we jumped on
the Time Machine and, with a great whirring of wheels,
observed the evolution of copyright from its origins in the
English censorship of the sixteenth century. I thought it well
to consult history if only to satisfy myself, and thereby my
audience, that as things were different in the past, they probably need not be as they are, and in any case will not remain
as they are very long. The historical exercise makes against
excessive conservatism, against timidity. The second lecture,
anatomizing the modern concepts of infringement, was a
means of reaching for the variables of policy that do or should
underlie copyright. In that analysis, and in the final lecture
considering the reform and future movement of the law, I
have treated copyright as not a single but a multiple subject
which best discloses its perplexities when it is examined piece
by piece rather than as a single whole. In the same sense I
have suggested that wise legislation will proceed not by deduc-
tion from a monistic premise but upon a series of judgments
about ends served and disserved by particular measures. Solutions should not be so rigid as to deny the future; they should

[106]Revision Bill § 601; *cf.* 1961 Report, *supra* note 54, at 119-24.

admit the variety and flux of experience and leave room for ready correction over time. Finally, I have introduced throughout a calculated amount of low-protectionist bias which I associate with a concern for easy public access to, and use and improvement of products of the mind.

For the opportunity to come back home to Columbia and vex the public air with some mildly unorthodox views about copyright, I give thanks to the generous impulse which long ago created the Carpentier Lectures. More embracingly, I want as an alumnus to express my lasting gratitude to the Columbia Law School, and to its Faculty—those brilliant individualists who, magically renewing themselves over the years, have with a certain loving asperity set the feet of generations of students firmly in the path of the law.

AN ADDED NOTE

The intermittency of the process of manufacturing the present book affords me an opportunity to carry the story of the revision effort a little further along and to record that, after painstaking work by its subcommittee led by Representative Kastenmeier, the House Judiciary Committee has reported the Revision Bill with a mixed bag of amendments.[107] The Bill is unchanged in general structure, but there are various changes of particulars. I shall only note some changes that bear on the producer-user questions discussed above.

1. There is no amendment dealing with photocopying or like reprographic techniques as such, but the "fair use" section

[107] See H. Rep. No. 2237, 89th Cong., 2d Sess. (dated 12 October 1966).

would be expanded on the lines of the similar provision of the 1964 draft bill.[108] The amended section refers to benign pur poses "such as criticism, comment, news reporting, teaching, scholarship, or research," and then lists a number of common-place factors—purpose of the use, nature of the work, etc.—that are to be considered in deciding the question of fairness.[109] In illustrating by means of homely examples the putative effects of the rewritten section, the House Report treats the situation of the classroom teacher rather sympathetically; but we are not spared the pious and cautious averments that the Committee has "no purpose of either freezing or changing the doctrine" of fair use and, again, that the section is "intended to restate the present judicial doctrine of fair use, not to change, narrow, or enlarge it in any way." Connected with the fair use provision is a clause allowing courts to remit "fixed" damages where an instructor in the course of face-to-face teaching activities infringes by reproducing a work in copies under a reasonable but mistaken belief that he is engaging in a fair use.[110] A new section, certainly welcome as far as it goes, would allow a nonprofit institution holding manuscripts or other unpublished works in an archival collection to reproduce them in facsimile for the purpose of preservation or for deposit for research use in another like institution.[111]

2. If a friendlier attitude toward fair use peeps through the Revision Bill as reported by the Committee, there is, on the other hand, an effective narrowing of the Bill's already guarded exemption of certain kinds of educational transmissions.[112] The

[108]See *supra* note 64.
[109]Reported Bill § 107.
[110]Reported Bill § 504(c)(2).
[111]Reported Bill § 108.
[112]See *supra* note 82.

exempted transmissions could now reach beyond classrooms to viewers who by reason of disability were unable to attend school, which is a useful advance; but the exemption would fail altogether if the radius of the area of transmission was more than one hundred miles, or if the time or content of the transmission was not controlled by the transmitting organization but depended on individual activation from an information storage and retrieval system or similar device.[113] Two cognate exemptions appearing in the Bill as introduced, for performances given at religious assemblies, or intended to raise money for education or other eleemosynary purposes, would also be narrowed.[114]

3. The Committee does not endorse the full-scale liability envisaged for CATV by the Revision Bill as introduced, but rather proceeds to classify the operations, actual and potential, of CATV systems to yield "white," "black," and "gray" results in regard to liability for the use of copyrighted works. The classification is intricate and need not be spelled out here. Operations constituting a mere "fill-in" service would be exempt, as where the system simply retransmits within the "area normally encompassed" by the primary transmitter. Operations supposed to damage the copyright owner directly by impairing his market would undergo full sanctions, as where the system originates programs or alters program content or imports signals into an area already "adequately served" in the sense of having full network coverage. Operations conceived to damage the copyright owner indirectly would subject the system to reasonable license fees (to be fixed by a court in the last re-

[113]Reported Bill § 110(2).
[114]Reported Bill § 110(3), (4); cf. Revision Bill as introduced, § 109(3), (4).

sort), as where the area served by the system does not receive all networks.[115]

4. The Committee would split the difference between the present two-cent compulsory music license and the three cents first proposed in the Revision Bill: it would adopt two and one-half cents as the base rate.[116]

Abandoning the effort to abolish completely the present jukebox exemption, the amended Bill would establish a compulsory license for the jukebox performance right at a base rate of three cents per work for each three-month period it was made available on the particular machine.[117]

[115]Reported Bill § 111(a)(3), (b), (c), (d).
[116]Reported Bill § 115(c)(2).
[117]Reported Bill § 116(c)(2).

Table of Cases Cited

Adams, case of, in RECORDS OF THE COURT OF THE STATIONERS' Co. 1602-1640, at 51, 83, 350, 351 (Jackson ed. 1957), 5

Addison-Wesley Pub. Co. v. Brown, 223 F. Supp. 219 (E.D.N.Y. 1963); 207 F. Supp. 678 (E.D.N.Y. 1962), 58

Alfred Bell & Co., Ltd. v. Catalda Fine Arts, Inc., 86 F. Supp. 399 (S.D.N.Y. 1949), aff'd, 191 F.2d 99 (2d Cir. 1951), 43, 45, 71

American Tobacco Co. v. Werckmeister, 207 U.S. 284 (1907), 86

Amsterdam v. Triangle Pub., Inc., 189 F.2d 104 (3d Cir. 1951), 63

Arnstein v. Edward B. Marks Music Corp., 82 F.2d 275 (2d Cir. 1936), 43

Aro Mfg. Co., Inc. v. Convertible Top Replacement Co., Inc., 377 U.S. 476 (1964), 95

Bach v. Longman, 2 Cowp. 623, 98 Eng. Rep. 1274 (K.B. 1777), 16

Baker v. Selden, 101 U.S. 99 (1879), 33, 63, 64, 65, 103

Barry v. Hughes, 103 F.2d 427 (2d Cir.), cert. denied, 308 U.S. 604 (1939), 72

Becker v. Loew's Inc., 133 F.2d 889 (7th Cir. 1943), 62

Beckford v. Hood, 7 T.R. 620, 101 Eng. Rep. 1164 (K.B. 1798), 26

Bell v. Whitehead, 3 Jur. 68 (Ch. 1839), 21

Benny v. Loew's Inc., 239 F.2d 532 (9th Cir. 1956), aff'd by an equally divided court, without opinion, sub nom. Columbia Broadcasting System, Inc. v. Loew's Inc., 356 U.S. 43 (1958), 69

Berlin v. E. C. Publications, Inc., 329 F.2d 541 (2d Cir), cert. denied, 379 U.S. 822 (1964), 58, 69

Bleistein v. Donaldson Lithographing Co., 188 U.S. 239 (1903), 34-35, 39, 45

Brady v. Daly, 175 U.S. 148 (1899), 31

Bramwell v. Halcomb, 2 My. & Cr. 737, 40 Eng. Rep. 1110 (Ch. 1836), 20

Broadway Music Corp. v. F-R Pub. Corp., 31 F. Supp. 817 (S.D.N.Y. 1940), 68

Brown Instrument Co. v. Warner, 161 F. 2d 910 (D.C. Cir. 1947), 65

Buck v. Jewell-LaSalle Realty Co., 283 U.S. 191 (1931), 104

Burnett v. Chetwood, 2 Mer. 441, 35 Eng. Rep. 1008 (Ch. 1720), 9-10

Cable Vision, Inc. v. KUTV, Inc., 335 F. 2d 348 (9th Cir. 1964), *cert. denied,* 379 U.S. 989 (1965), *rev'g* 211 F. Supp. 47 (S.D. Idaho 1962), 96, 105

Capitol Records, Inc. v. Mercury Records Corp., 221 F. 2d 657 (2d Cir. 1955), 39, 89-93, 95, 99, 109

Carnan v. Bowles, 2 Bro. C.C. 80, 29 Eng. Rep. 45 (Ch. 1786), 19

Cary v. Faden, 5 Ves. Jun. 24, 31 Eng. Rep. 453 (Ch. 1799), 19

Cary v. Kearsley, 4 Esp. 168, 170 Eng. Rep. 679 (K.B. 1802), 19

Cary v. Longman, 1 East 358, 102 Eng. Rep. 138 (K.B. 1801), 19

Cheney Bros. v. Doris Silk Corp., 35 F. 2d 279 (2d Cir. 1929), *cert. denied,* 281 U.S. 728 (1930), 87-88, 89

Clayton v. Stone, 5 Fed. Cas. 999 (No. 2872) (C.C.S.D.N.Y. 1829), 33

Columbia Broadcasting System v. Teleprompter Corp., 148 U.S.P.Q. 417 (S.D.N.Y. 1965), 105

Columbia Pictures Corp. v. National Broadcasting Co., 137 F. Supp. 348 (S.D.Cal. 1955), 69

Compco Corp. v. Day-Brite Lighting, Inc., 376 U.S. 234 (1964), 93-95, 98

Continental Casualty Co. v. Beardsley, 253 F.2d 702 (2d Cir.), *cert. denied,* 358 U.S. 816 (1958), *modifying* 151 F. Supp. 28 (S.D.N.Y. 1957), 64-65

D'Almaine v. Boosey, 1 Y. & C. Ex. 288, 160 Eng. Rep. 117 (Ex. 1835), 8, 20-21, 31

Daly v. Palmer, 6 Fed. Cas. 1132 (No. 3552) (C.C.S.D.N.Y. 1868), 31-32, 47

Daly v. Webster, 56 Fed. 483 (2d Cir. 1892), 31

Davies v. Bowes, 209 Fed. 53 (S.D.N.Y. 1913), *aff'd*, 219 Fed. 178 (2d Cir. 1914), 60

Davis v. E. I. du Pont de Nemours & Co., 240 F. Supp. 612 (S.D.N.Y. 1965); 249 F. Supp. 471 (S.D.N.Y. 1966), 50, 74

De Acosta v. Brown, 146 F.2d 408 (2d Cir. 1944), *cert. denied*, 325 U.S. 862 (1945), 72-73

De Silva Construction Corp. v. Herrald, 213 F. Supp. 184 (M.D.Fla. 1962), 66, 86

Detective Comics, Inc. v. Bruns Pub., Inc., 111 F.2D 432 (2d Cir. 1940), 44, 51

Dodsley v. Kinnersley, Amb. 403, 27 Eng. Rep. 270 (Ch. 1761), 11

Donaldson v. Becket, 2 Bro. P.C. 129, 1 Eng. Rep. 937, 4 Burr. 2408, 98 Eng. Rep. 257 (H.L. 1774), 17 HANSARD, PARLIAMENTARY HISTORY OF ENGLAND 953-1003 (1813), 7, 8, 14-16, 92, 95

Edgar H. Wood Assoc. v. Skene, 347 Mass. 351, 197 N.E.2d 886 (1964), 66, 86

Eisenschiml v. Fawcett Pub., Inc., 246 F.2d 598 (7th Cir.), *cert. denied*, 355 U.S. 907 (1957), 62

Emerson v. Davies, 8 Fed. Cas. 615 (No. 4436) (C.C.D.Mass. 1845), 27, 28, 29, 52

Erie R.R. v. Tompkins, 304 U.S. 64 (1938), 89, 90

Fashion Originators Guild v. FTC, 114 F.2d 80 (2d Cir. 1940), *aff'd*, 312 U.S. 457 (1941), 88

Ferris v. Frohman, 223 U.S. 424 (1912), 84-85, 95

Fisher v. Star Co., 231 N.Y. 414, 132 N.E. 133, *cert. denied*, 257 U.S. 654 (1921), 95

Folsom v. Marsh, 9 Fed. Cas. 342 (No. 4901) (C.C.D.Mass. 1841), 27, 28, 67

Fred Fisher, Inc. v. Dillingham, 298 Fed. 45 (S.D.N.Y. 1924), 42-43, 73

Fred Fisher Music Co. v. M. Witmark & Sons, 318 U.S. 643 (1943), 8, 112

Gray v. Russell, 10 Fed. Cas. 1035 (No. 5728) (C.C.D.Mass. 1839), 20, 27, 28

Gyles v. Wilcox, 2 Atk. 141, 3 Atk. 269, 26 Eng. Rep. 489, 957; Barn. Ch. 368, 27 Eng. Rep. 682 (Ch. 1740), 10-11

Haas v. Leo Feist, Inc., 234 Fed. 105 (S.D.N.Y. 1916), 70, 72

Hammond, C. S. & Co. v. International College Globe, Inc., 210 F. Supp. 206 (S.D.N.Y. 1962), 63

Heim v. Universal Pictures Co., Inc., 154 F.2d 480 (2nd Cir. 1946), 46

Hein v. Harris, 175 Fed. 875 (C.C.S.D.N.Y. 1910), *aff'd,* 183 Fed. 107 (2d Cir. 1910), 30, 41-42, 43

Henderson v. Tompkins, 60 Fed. 758 (C.C.D.Mass. 1894), 30

Henry Holt & Co., Inc. v. Liggett & Myers Tobacco Co., 23 F. Supp. 302 (E.D.Pa. 1938), 68

Holdredge v. Knight Pub. Corp., 214 F. Supp. 921 (S.D.Cal. 1963), 62

Ideal Toy Corp. v. Sayco Doll Corp., 302 F.2d 623 (2d Cir. 1962), 55

Intermountain Broadcasting & Television Corp. v. Idaho Microwave, Inc., 196 F. Supp. 315 (S.D.Idaho 1961), 105

International News Service v. Associated Press, 248 U.S. 215 (1918), 34, 60, 61, 86-89, 90, 95

Jaggard, case of, in RECORDS OF THE COURT OF THE STATIONERS' CO. 1602-1640, at 178, 204, 326, 327, 328, 334, 335 (Jackson ed. 1957), 5

Jewelers' Circ. Pub. Co. v. Keystone Pub. Co., 274 Fed. 932 (S.D.N.Y. 1921), *aff'd,* 281 Fed. 83 (2d Cir.), *cert. denied,* 259 U.S. 581 (1922), 58, 59

Jollie v. Jaques, 3 Fed. Cas. 910 (No. 7437) (C.C.S.D.N.Y. 1850), 30

Kalem Co. v. Harper Bros., 222 U.S. 55 (1911), 35-36

Kelly v. Hooper, 1 Y. & C.C.C. 197, 62 Eng. Rep. 852 (1841), 20

King v. Mister Maestro, Inc., 224 F. Supp. 101 (S.D.N.Y. 1963), 85

Kolbe, H. M. Co., Inc. v. Armgus Textile Co., Inc., 315 F.2d 70 (2d Cir. 1963), 81

Korzybski v. Underwood & Underwood, Inc., 36 F.2d 727 (2d Cir. 1929), 65

Lawrence v. Dana, 15 Fed. Cas. 6 (No. 8136) (C.C.D.Mass. 1869), 67

Lewis v. Fullarton, 2 Beav. 6, 48 Eng. Rep. 1080 (Ch. 1839), 20

Life Music, Inc. v. Wonderland Music Co., 241 F. Supp. 653 (S.D.N.Y. 1965), 46

Longman v. Winchester, 16 Ves. Jun. 269, 33 Eng. Rep. 987 (Ch. 1809), 19

MacDonald v. DuMaurier, 144 F.2d 696 (2d Cir. 1944), 50

Martin v. Wright, 6 Sim. 297, 58 Eng. Rep. 605 (Ch. 1833), 21

Matthewson v. Stockdale, 12 Ves. Jun. 270, 33 Eng. Rep. 103 (Ch. 1806), 18, 19

Mawman v. Tegg, 2 Russ. 385, 38 Eng. Rep. 380 (Ch. 1826), 20

May v. Bray, 30 C.O. Bull. 435 (S.D.Cal. 1955), 66

Mazer v. Stein, 347 U.S. 201 (1954), 39, 54, 55, 56, 64, 88

Metropolitan Opera Ass'n, Inc. v. Wagner-Nichols Recorder Corp., 199 Misc. 786, 101 N.Y.S.2d 483 (Sup. Ct. 1950), *aff'd per curiam,* 279 App. Div. 632, 107 N.Y.S.2d 795 (1951), 90

Millar v. Taylor, 4 Burr. 2303, 98 Eng. Rep. 201 (K.B. 1796), 12, 13-14, 15, 92

Mott, J. L. Iron Works v. Clow, 82 Fed. 316 (7th Cir. 1897), 33

Muller v. Triborough Bridge Authority, 43 F. Supp. 298 (S.D.N.Y. 1942), 66

Murray v. Bogue, 1 Drew. 353, 61 Eng. Rep. 487 (Ch. 1852), 22

Myers v. The Mail & Express Co., No. E-15-138, S.D.N.Y., 23 July 1919, 61-62

National Comics Pub., Inc. v. Fawcett Pub., Inc., 191 F.2d 594 (2d Cir. 1951), 46, 51-52

National Tel. News Co. v. Western Union Tel. Co., 119 Fed. 294 (7th Cir. 1902), 34, 60

Newbery's Case, Lofft 775, 98 Eng. Rep. 913 (Ch. 1773), 11-12, 18

Nichols v. Loder, 2 Coop. T. Cott. 217, 47 Eng. Rep. 1135 (Ch. 1831), 20

Nichols v. Universal Pictures Corp., 45 F.2d 119 (2d Cir. 1930), *cert. denied,* 282 U.S. 902 (1931), 46-48, 50, 56, 67

Orgel v. Clark Boardman Co., Ltd., 301 F.2d 119 (2d Cir.), *cert. denied,* 371 U.S. 817 (1962), *modifying* 128 U.S.P.Q. 531 (S.D.N.Y. 1960), 71

Peter Pan Fabrics, Inc. v. Martin Weiner Corp., 274 F.2d 487 (2d
    Cir. 1960), 54, 81
Pierce & Bushnell Mfg. Co. v. Werckmeister, 72 Fed. 54 (1st Cir.
    1896), 86
Pottstown Daily News Pub. Co. v. Pottstown Broadcasting Co., 411
    Pa. 383, 192 A.2d 657 (1963); 247 F. Supp. 578 (E.D.Pa. 1965),
    95
Public Affairs Associates, Inc. v. Rickover, 284 F.2d 262 (D.C.Cir.
    1960), *vacated for insufficient record,* 369 U.S. 111 (1962), 61
R.C.A. Mfg. Co., Inc. v. Whiteman, 114 F.2d 86 (2d Cir.), *cert.
    denied,* 311 U.S. 712 (1940), 88, 89, 109
Reiss v. National Quotation Bureau, Inc., 276 Fed. 717 (S.D.N.Y.
    1921), 53
Ricordi, G. & Co. v. Haendler, 194 F.2d 914 (2d Cir. 1952), 90
Rosemont Enterprises, Inc. v. Random House, Inc., 2d Cir., 17 August
    1966, *rev'g* 150 U.S.P.Q. 367 (S.D.N.Y. 1966), 62, 73
Roworth v. Wilkes, 1 Camp. 94, 170 Eng. Rep. 889 (K.B. 1807), 20
Saunders v. Smith, 3 My. & Cr. 711, 40 Eng. Rep. 1100 (Ch. 1838),
    21
Sayre v. Moore, 1 East 361 n., 102 Eng. Rep. 139 n. (K.B. 1785), 16-
    18
Sears, Roebuck & Co. v. Stiffel Co., 376 U.S. 225 (1964), 93-95, 98
Seltzer v. Sunbrock, 22 F. Supp. 621 (S.D.Cal. 1938), 63
Shapiro, Bernstein & Co., Inc. v. H. L. Green Co., Inc., 316 F.2d 304
    (2d Cir. 1963), 73
Sheldon v. Metro-Goldwyn Pictures Corp., 81 F.2d 49 (2d Cir.), *cert.
    denied,* 298 U.S. 669 (1936), *rev'g* 7 F. Supp. 837 (S.D.N.Y.
    1934) (on liability); 106 F.2d 45 (2nd Cir. 1939), *aff'd,* 309 U.S.
    390 (1940) (on accounting), 1-2, 36, 44, 48-50, 56, 67, 70-71
Stodart v. Mutual Film Corp., 249 Fed. 507 (S.D.N.Y. 1917), *aff'd,*
    249 Fed. 513 (2d Cir. 1918), 41
Story's Executors v. Holcomb, 23 Fed. Cas. 171 (No. 13497)
    (C.C.D.Ohio 1847), 29
Stowe v. Thomas, 23 Fed. Cas. 201 (No. 13514) (C.C.E.D.Pa.
    1853), 29-30

Taylor Instrument Cos. v. Fawley-Brost Co., 139 F.2d 98 (7th Cir. 1943), *cert. denied,* 321 U.S. 785 (1944), 65

Toksvig v. Bruce Pub. Co., 181 F.2d 664 (7th Cir. 1950), 62

Tonson v. Collins, 1 Black. W. 301, 96 Eng. Rep. 169 (K.B. 1761), 13, 15

Tonson v. Walker (Ch. 1739), referred to at 4 Burr. 2325, 98 Eng. Rep. 213, 13

Tonson v. Walker, 3 Swans. 672, 36 Eng. Rep. 1017 (Ch. 1752), 11, 13

Triangle Pub., Inc. v. New England Newspaper Pub. Co., 46 F. Supp. 198 (D.Mass. 1942), 61

Tribune Co. of Chicago v. Associated Press, 116 Fed. 126 (C.C.N.D.Ill. 1900), 34

Trusler v. Murray, 1 East 362 n., 102 Eng. Rep. 140 n. (K.B. 1789), 18

United Artists Television, Inc. v. Fortnightly Corp., 149 U.S.P.Q. 758 (S.D.N.Y. 1966), 105

Walter v. Lane, [1900] A.C. 539, 45

Warner Bros. Pictures, Inc. v. Columbia Broadcasting System, Inc., 216 F.2d 945 (9th Cir. 1954), *cert. denied,* 348 U.S. 971 (1955), 51

Washingtonian Publishing Co., Inc. v. Pearson, 306 U.S. 30 (1939), 82

Werckmeister v. American Lithographic Co., 134 Fed. 321 (2d Cir. 1904), 86

West v. Francis, 5 B. & Ald. 737, 106 Eng. Rep. 1361 (K.B. 1822), 20

Wheaton v. Peters, 33 U.S. (8 Pet.) 591 (1834), 26-27, 80

White-Smith Music Pub. Co. v. Apollo Co., 209 U.S. 1 (1908), 35, 108

Whittingham v. Wooler, 2 Swans. 428, 36 Eng. Rep. 679 (Ch. 1817), 22

Wilkins v. Aikin, 17 Ves. Jun. 422, 34 Eng. Rep. 163 (Ch. 1810), 21

Wrench v. Universal Pictures Co., Inc., 104 F. Supp. 374 (S.D.N.Y. 1952), 82

Wyatt v. Barnard, 3 Ves. & B. 77, 35 Eng. Rep. 408 (Ch. 1814), 22

Index

Abinger, Chief Baron, 8, 21
Abridgments, 10-12, 14, 15, 16, 22, 29, 40, 62, 100
Adaptations, 40
Addison, 8
Administrative agency, to assist in copyright regulation, 110-11
Advertisements, 33, 34
American Council of Learned Societies, views of, 116
Anticipation, as defense to infringement, see Prior art
Apparel, configuration of, 55-56, 65-66
Apsley, Chancellor, 8, 11
Architect's plans, 65-66, 85-86
Aristotle, 72
Arithmetics, 27
Arrangements: of existing material as justifying copyright, 28, 40; musical, 100
ASCAP, 102
Assignment of copyright, 8
Aston, Justice, 13, 15, 29

Bacon, Francis, 24
Baldwin, Justice, 26
Beljame, A., 23
Bender, P., 94
Berne Convention, 123
Biographies, see Histories

Birrell, A., 5
Black, Justice, 93, 95
Blackstone, 11, 15
Blount, C., 6
Bradley, Justice, 33
Brandeis, Justice, 86, 89, 94
Brown, R. S., Jr., 90, 94

Camden, Lord, 6, 15
Carter, Judge, 69
Cartoons, 51-52
Caxton, 2
Censorship, 3-4, 6
Chafee, Z., Jr., 38, 111, 115
Characters, 48, 50-52
Clark, Judge C. E., 50, 55
Clarke, Master of the Rolls, 11
Clarke, T. W., 32
Clearance at source, 122
Clifford, Justice, 67
Commerce power, 92
Common-law copyright, 84; see Perpetual copyright; State and national power over copyright; Unpublished works
Community antenna television (CATV), 104-6, 127
Competition, 55, 95, 106
Compilations, 18, 34, 43
Compulsory license: in general, 73, 110, 111; for sound recordings,

38-39, 108-9, 128; proposed for certain CATV operations, 127; for jukebox performances, 128
Computers, 65, 102-4, 118-23
Comsat, 119
Constitutional problems, 25, 33, 36, 39, 43, 64, 69, 75, 91-95
Copy, stationers' right of, 4-5
Copying: as essential to infringement, 41-43; unconscious, 42, 46, 72-73; see Prior art
Copyright: nature and purposes, 7-8, 34, 35, 41-43, 45, 73, 74-78, 80, 117-22; see Common-law copyright; Patent law
Copyright Act of 1909, 38-41, 89
Copyrightability, and plagiarism, 38
Criticism, quotation for purpose of, 21, 69

Damages and profits, on account of infringement, 70-74
Dance, 97
DeGrey, Chief Justice, 15
Deposit of specimen copies, 79, 81
Derenberg, W., 93, 94
Derivative works, 40, 56-57, 100
Design patent, 54, 93
Dictionaries, 17, 59
Directories, 18, 19, 59, 60
Douglas, Justice, 56
Dramatic works, 31-32, 33, 40, 46-51
Dramatizations, 32, 36, 40, 57, 100
Drone, E. S., 115
Dryden, 23
Duration of copyright, 7, 40, 111-17; see Perpetual copyright

Early Bird satellite, 119, 122
Educational uses of copyrighted works, 106-8, 118, 126-27
Eldon, Chancellor, 19, 21, 28, 37

Entry, in register of Stationers' Company, 4-5
Equality, of copyright burdens, 104-5
Equivalents, doctrine of in patent law, 32
Erskine, Chancellor, 19
Exemptions, from copyright burdens, 99, 101, 106-8, 110
Explanation, distinguished from utilization, 33, 54, 65, 103; see Systems and schemes
Expression, see Form or expression

Fact works, 17-20, 27-28, 30, 33, 58-61, 67, 77
Fair use, 17, 21, 28, 67-70, 102, 125-26
Federal Communications Commission (FCC), regulation of CATV, 105-6
Feinberg, Judge, 74
Fictionalization, 100
First 350 Years, The: origins of copyright in official censorship, 2-3; Stationers' Company, 3-6; emancipation of press, 6; Statute of Anne, 7-9; scope of protection of works in early cases—translations, 9-10, abridgments, 10-12; scope of protection envisaged during argument over perpetual copyright, 12-17; enlargement of protection, 17-22; Romantic revival, 22-25; U.S. Constitution and early legislation, 25; renewal of question of perpetual copyright, 26-27; importation and elaboration of English doctrine by Story, 27-28; later doctrine, 29-32; statutory changes, 32; questions of copyrightability of systems, news, etc., 32-34; Holmes's attempt at generalization, 34-36.

Fixation of works, 97-98

Foreign works, 122-23

Formalities, 26-27, 38, 79, 80-83; *see* Deposit of specimen copies; Notice of copyright; Recordation of copyright transfers; Registration of copyright

Form or expression, distinguished from idea or substance, 9, 11, 14, 16, 17, 19, 20, 32, 35, 36, 47ff., 65

Forms and blanks, copyrightability of, 33, 64-65

Fragility of works, in relation to copyrightability and infringement, 7-8, 55, 74

Frank, Judge, 43, 45

Future of copyright, 117-22

Gorman, R. A., 58, 59, 60, 63, 67

Government works, 121

Grammars, 27

Graphic works, 20, 30, 34, 39, 54-56

Gray, J. C., 32

Grier, Justice, 29, 30, 32

Grosscup, Judge, 34, 60

Gutenberg, 1, 118

Hand, Judge Learned, 1, Lecture II *passim*, 87-92, 95

Handler, M., 94

Hardwicke, Chancellor, 10, 11

Herlands, Judge, 105

Histories, 18, 21, 27, 28, 61-62

History of copyright, *see* First 350 Years

Holmes, Justice, 34-36, 39, 45, 58, 86, 95

Horace, 23

Hume, David, 15

Idea, *see* Form or expression

Imitation, classical view of permissible, 23-24

Improvement of work, as avoiding infringement, 16-17, 18, 49-50

Incentive, copyright as, 7-8, 25, 74-75, 121

Indexes and abstracts, 69, 100, 120

Informational works, *see* Fact works

Infringement, *see* Plagiarism

Injunction, 73

International copyright, 122-24

Invention, *see* Originality and Novelty; Patent Law

Johnson, Samuel, 15

Joint works, 117-18

Jones, Glyn, 69

Jukebox exemption, 101, 128

Justice Department, views of, 56, 106

Kaplan, B., 51, 85, 90, 92

Kastenmeier, Representative, 125

Keats, 23

Kenyon, Chief Justice, 18

Kocourek, A., 87

Latman, A. K., 68

Leeds, D., 94

Lieber, F., 115

Macaulay, 6, 115

Macclesfield, Chancellor, 10

MacDiarmid, H., 68-69

McKenna, Justice, 86

McLean, Justice, 29, 32

McLuhan, M., 118

Madison, 25

Mansfield, Chief Justice, Lecture I *passim*, 50

Manufacturing clause, 38, 123-24

Maps, 16-17, 21, 62-63

Marx, Karl, 116

Merger, of electronic companies and publishers, 119

Misappropriation, *see* Unfair competition

Monopoly, 8, 36, 75, 114
Moral rights, 13, 78, 120
Motion pictures, 35-36, 56
Music, 16, 20-21, 35, 40, 41-43, 53,
  118

National power over copyright, see
  State and national power
Natural rights, 2, 80
News, 33-34, 39, 59-61
Nimmer, M. B., 27, 46, 85, 111
Notice of copyright, 38, 63, 79, 81-
  82
Novelization, 40
Novels, 30, 36, 52
Novelty, see Originality and Novelty

Originality and novelty, 24, 31, 34,
  41-44, 58, 77, 97, 117
Ornamental designs, 54-56; see
  Graphic works
Overhage, C. F. J., 118

Pantomime, 36, 97
Parody, 69, 109; see Fair use
Passing off, see Unfair competition
Patent law, 15, 29-30, 31, 32, 33,
  41, 54, 65, 103
Patents for books, 3, 4
Patronage, 22
Patterning, as aid in determining
  plagiarism, 48-50, 52-56, 77; see
  Form or expression
Performance rights, attaching to cer-
  tain works, 31, 40, 64, 105
Performer's rights, 88-91, 97, 109,
  118; see Sound recordings
Perpetual copyright ("The Question
  of Literary Property"), 12-16, 26,
  95
Personality, see Copyright: nature
  and purposes
Phonorecords, see Sound recordings

Photocopying, 68, 101-02, 125; see
  Fair use
Photographs, 61
Piracy, see Plagiarism
Plagiarism Reexamined: term taken
  to include piracy and extend generally to infringement, 38; related
  to copyrightability, 38; provisions
  of act of 1909, 38-41; copying as
  essential to plagiarism, 41-44; elements too small or too large to
  admit of plagiarism, 45-47; patterning as aid in determining
  plagiarism, 47-49; permissible use
  of work, effect of improvement,
  49, 57-58; dramatic works, 48-49;
  characters, 50-52; novels, 52;
  treatises, 52; music, 53; graphic
  works, 54-56; derivative works,
  56-58; fact works, 58-63; systems,
  practical utilizations, architect's
  plans, 63-66; fair use, 67-70;
  remedies—apportionment of profits, effects of innocence, 70-74;
  general considerations, 74-78; see
  also 99-100, 103; First 350 Years;
  Form or expression
Plan of work, as copyrightable element, 28, 31, 33
Plot, as copyrightable element, 30-
  32, 47-52
Preemption, of state law by copyright act or Constitution, 89-96;
  see Constitutional problems
Press, emancipation of, 6
Prints or labels, 45
Prior art, 30, 31, 41, 44
Privacy, see Copyright: nature and
  purposes
Profits, see Damages and profits
Proposals and Prospects: objectives
  of revision of law, 79; Revision
  Bill, 79-80; formalities, 80-83; un-
  principled extension of protection

by distortion of "publication," 83-85; by doctrines of "unfair competition," 86-89, with resulting preemption issues, 89-96; proposed solutions, 96-99; ascription and modulation of rights to settle producer-user problems, 99-101; photocopying, 101-2; computers, 102-4; CATV, 104-6; educational uses, 106-8; sound recordings, 108-9; general comment, question of administrative agency for copyright, 109-11; duration of copyright and reversion of rights, 111-117; future of copyright, 117-22; international copyright, 122-24; recapitulation, 124-25; added note on Revision Bill as reported, 125-28

Public domain, 60, 96

Publication, 12, 27, 83-85, 96-99

Recordation, of transfers of copyright, 79, 81

Registration of copyright, 7, 26, 38, 79, 82-83

Remedies, 38, 63, 73-74, 109; *see* Damages and profits; Injunction

Renewal of copyright, 38, 40, 112; *see* Reversion of rights

Renouard, 115

Reprographic technology, 102

Reversion of rights to author, 8, 113-14; *see* Renewal of copyright

Revision Bill of 1965: as introduced, 79-80, 82, 83, 96-111, 112-17; as reported by House Committee, 125-28

Roadbooks, 19

Romanticism, affecting notions of plagiarism, 22-25, 34, 43, 117

Rovere, R. H., 60

Scrutton, T. E., 20

Setting, 51

Shelley, 23

Sound recordings, 85, 88, 97, 100, 108-09; *see* Compulsory license; Performer's rights; Publication

Stage effects, 31

Star Chamber, 3, 36

State and national power over copyright, 89-99; *see* Constitutional problems; Preemption

Stationers' Company, 3-6, 36

Statute of Anne (1710), 7-9, 36

Steele, 8

Story, Justice, 20, 27-28, 29, 31, 37, 52

Strahan, W., 15

Subject matter of copyright, 39, 97-98, 100; *see under* Dramatic works, Novels, etc.

Supplementary works, 100

Swift, 8

Systems and schemes, 33, 63-65, 103

Talfourd, Sergeant, 115

Technology and copyright, 1, 79, 101ff., 117-22

Thompson, Justice, 26

Titles, 46

Translations, 9-10, 14, 15, 16, 22, 29-30, 32, 40, 100

Treatises and textbooks, 18, 28, 52

Typographical works, 99

Unfair competition, 50, 57, 60, 86-95, 98

Uniformity, as aim of copyright power, 91; *see* Constitutional problems

Universal Copyright Convention, 123

Unpublished works, 12, 84-85, 98-99, 115-16, 126

Use of work, distinct from plagiarism, 14, 49, 57-58, 68

U.S.S.R., 123

Versions, 40
Voltaire, 78

Warburton, Bishop, 15
Washington, Judge, 61
Whitgift, Archbishop, 3, 36
Willes, Justice, 13, 29
Works for hire, 113-14

Works of art, *see* Graphic works
Wyzanski, Judge, 161

Yates, Justice, 14
Young, Edward, 23, 37

Zimmerman, E. M., 106

www.ingramcontent.com/pod-product-compliance
Lightning Source LLC
Chambersburg PA
CBHW021600210326
41599CB00010B/535